PRIEST AND BEGGAR

Kevin Wells

Priest and Beggar

The Heroic Life of
Venerable Aloysius Schwartz

IGNATIUS PRESS   SAN FRANCISCO

Cover photograph:
Aloysius Schwartz and Orphans at the Construction of Busan Boystown (1971)
Courtesy of the Sisters of Mary

Cover design by Enrique J. Aguilar

© 2021 by Ignatius Press, San Francisco
All rights reserved
ISBN 978-1-62164-506-1 (PB)
ISBN 978-1-64229-168-1 (eBook)
Library of Congress Control Number 2021931406
Printed in the United States of America ∞

*This book is dedicated to little Brian Christopher Wert,
the seed who died and raised an incomprehensible
harvest. Brian, your heart beats still through the
holy work of the Sisters of Mary.*

À la Vierge des Pauvres [To the Virgin of the Poor]:

For a long time now I have entrusted to you all that I have & all that I am. You have taken all, I have nothing. *Je suis pauvre* [I am poor].

My health you have taken.

My good name you have taken. I am now counted among the disobedient or psychotics or fools. I do not think I exaggerate.

My country (Korea) you have torn from me.

My mission vocation seems to be lost.

My friends for the most part leave me to my own devices.

Materially I have little.

O Vierge des Pauvres, je vous remercie. J'ai voulu la pauvrité et elle m'embrase forcement. [O Virgin of the Poor, I thank you. I wanted poverty, and it embraces me fiercely.]

Vierge, non, je ne te donne rien. Tu m'as fait cadeau de la pauvrité et de la souffrance [Virgin, no, I give you nothing. You have given me the gift of poverty and suffering] & by these two pearls I am ground into a host.

O Mary, I dare not say I have nothing more to give or what remains (I do not know) will be torn from me as a limb.

I renew—so deeply conscious of what I am, my weakness, my imperfection—the words of consecration: all I have and am—*oui! Vierge des Pauvres, oui, oui! Mais, O Mère, pitié, ego sum pauper et solus, et je suis si las.* [Virgin of the Poor, yes, yes! But O Mother, have pity, I am a beggar and alone, and I am so weary.] But I will risk all, all, all.

O Vierge des Pauvres, ayez pitié de moi. Voyiez mes larmes—pitié, pitié, pitié. [O Virgin of the Poor, have pity on me. Look at my tears, have pity, have pity, have pity.]

Aloysius Schwartz
Prêtre et Pauper [Priest and Beggar]

Dec 31, 1958
Kyoto, Japan

à la Vierge des Pauvres:

For a longtime now I have entrusted to you all that I have + all that I am. You have taken all, I have nothing. Je suis Pauvre.

My health you have taken.

My good name you have taken. I am now counted among the disobedient or psychotics or fools. I do not think I exaggerate.

My country (Korea) you have torn from me.

My mission vocation seems to be lost.

My friends for the most part leave me to my own devices.

Materially I have little.

O Vierge des Pauvres, je vous remercie. J'ai voulu la pauvreté et elle m'embrasse férocement.

Vierge, non, je ne te donne rien. Tu m'as fait cadeau de la pauvreté et de la souffrance + by these two pearls I am ground into a host.

O Mary, I dare not say I have nothing more to give or what remains (I do not know) will be torn from me as a limb.

I renew — so deeply conscious of what I am, my weakness, my imperfection — the words of consecration: all I have and am — oui! Vierge des Pauvres, oui, oui. Mais, o mère, pitié, ego sum pauper et solus, et je suis si las. But I will risk all, all, all.

O Vierge des Pauvres, ayez pitié de moi. Voyez mes larmes, pitié, pitié, pitié.

Aloysius Schwartz
Petre et Pauper

CONTENTS

ACKNOWLEDGMENTS

Many have assisted with this work. I am indebted to the Sisters of Mary religious community and to Sherlyn Comia, who offered old stories, memories, and an intimate knowledge and grasp of Father Al's life and mission. Father Dan Leary, who stepped into the shoes of a giant as the Sisters of Mary's chaplain, was encouraging throughout the journey. Father Al's brother, Lou Schwartz, who died in January 2021, was my greatest friend throughout my research on those early years; I will dearly miss our lively talks and correspondence. Also, thanks go to Father Al's youngest sister, Joan Baur, for her memories and storytelling. I'm grateful to Monsignor James Golasinski; the hour-long phone calls opened doors, chapters, and revelations. The excellent editorial team at Ignatius was a true joy to work alongside. Thanks to Father Joseph Fessio for identifying the remarkable story of Father Al and inviting this biography into the fold. To Damiano Park, I know why Father Al chose you as his wingman; thank you for taking me into those tough early days in Busan.

I am especially appreciative of the Sisters of Mary President Paul Gesterling and of Tom and Glory Sullivan and Steve Peroutka for inviting me to the challenge of bringing this Commando onto the pages of a book. Bethany Meola, as is her custom, proved exceptional with her editing. Kindly help was given by Jennifer Brinker and Bill Quinn, who were good to me at various points of this process. Jeff Phillips, thanks for the writing getaway in the Pennsylvania coal mines—and thanks to my siblings who gave me a quiet spot to write by the ocean. And special thanks to my family—Krista, Gabrielle, Sean, and Shannon—for giving me the office to dig up the holy grave of Venerable Al. It was a providential escape from the year of 2020.

Kevin Wells
March 1, 2021

ABBREVIATIONS

Abbreviations have generally been used to cite sources in the footnotes:

DJ   *Dans la joie du Seigneur: In the Joy of the Lord, Aloysius Schwartz.* Silang, Philippines: FACFI, 2016.

FA   *Fully Alive! Celebrating the Story of Fr. Aloysius Schwartz and 25 Years of the Sisters of Mary in the Philippines.* Silang, Philippines: FACFI, 2010.

Glow   *Glow! God's Light Outspoken through the Words of Venerable Aloysius Schwartz.* Private publication, Sisters of Mary, undated.

KMS   Schwartz, Aloysius. *Killing Me Softly: The Inspiring Story of a Champion of the Poor.* New York: Alba House, 1993.

PM   Schwartz, Aloysius. Personal Manuscripts and Archives. Sisters of Mary, Silang, Philippines.

Pos   Congregation for the Causes of Saints. *Beatificationis et Canonizationis Servi Dei Aloisii Schwartz: Positio Super Vita, Virtutibus et Fama Sanctitatis.* Rome: Vatican, 2012.

Pov   Schwartz, Aloysius. *Poverty: Sign of Our Times.* New York: Alba House, 1970.

Serm   *Sermons by Msgr. Aloysius Schwartz.* Vols. 1–9. Private publication, Sisters of Mary, undated.

StSi   Schwartz, Aloysius. *The Starved and the Silent.* New York: Doubleday, 1966.

TL   Schwartz, Aloysius. *To Live Is Christ: The Sisters of Mary Book of Spirituality.* Rockville, Md.: Government Institutes, 1991.

PROLOGUE

I WAS DEEP into the Mexican interior on a long and radio-less car ride from Guadalajara to Chalco, passing through land lonely as Gethsemane. My traveling companions were tired and silent as we passed brushfires high up on mountains, lonesome haciendas, and sombreroed cowboys minding slender cattle. As I moved through that quiet place, my mind traveled to what I'd absorbed the previous two weeks at Chalco Girlstown, a free Catholic boarding school for poor and neglected children, dropped into the center of a hard-luck village outside Mexico City. I'd seen things people no longer see; I'd witnessed what seemed to be miracles. As we drove on, my focus settled on a single thought Sister Margie Cheong shared, just as she finished a Rosary walk at nightfall: "Time here is like Magdalene's perfume; it is precious for us. We give all we have and are to them."

The teenagers at this school blaze with a startling type of joy. It is not a fallow, painted-on joy, but one built firmly on what they interiorly know—the Sisters of Mary have surrendered their lives for them. One night, I saw hundreds of girls press into the gymnasium for evening catechism as a blood-red sun set against two snow-capped volcanoes in the distance. An hour later, they poured back out of the doors, smiling, waving, and welcoming me, the stranger in their midst. The volcanoes seemed to stand prouder, like watchful fathers seeing their daughters off to bed. It would have been okay if time had stopped right then.

Visitors to Chalco are lifted into a different dimension, into a way of life that's disappearing in America. The 3,142 teenage girls at Chalco Girlstown, like the 1,910 teenage boys at its brother Boystown in Guadalajara, are without cell phones or earbuds. Each evening at seven P.M., they pray the Rosary together, in a chorus that reverberates like thousands of bees. Because they do not play video games or browse social media, they have more time to hone their God-given skills. For decades, their high school sports teams have routinely won national championships. After graduating, classical musicians join orchestras where they play before thousands. These are formed, joyful Catholics. A good number enter into religious life.

Many children at this Girlstown and at the Guadalajara school have worked fields barefoot since the age of eight or nine, often returning home to find no food on the table. Almost all have felt the fear of not knowing the whereabouts of their next meal. Zayra, one of the children I met, told me that she was once chased an hour up a mountain by a human trafficker, her village by the sea being full of such monsters. Her grandfather, with whom she lived, was drunk most nights. "I would kneel in front of the statue of Mary", she said, "and pray the fights and drinking would stop." Another girl, Antonina, has been an orphan since her father was shot dead in the street; her mom, she believes, burned to death. These stories—there are thousands— are why the Sisters of Mary welcome the children each morning as mothers do sons returning from war.

These are saving grounds, fields of goodwill and rebirth. It took me a while to figure out why the teenagers addressed each of the Sisters as *madre*, not *hermana*. But these faithful women educate, nourish, counsel, catechize, jog with, play sports with, and pray with the students; they never stop. "We are spiritual mothers to them first", one sister told me. "They have been through too much." The slow, tender eloquence of their maternal love pulls away layer after layer of wounds and horrors too graphic for this writing—and allows them to mend. Their blood loyalty has a singular aim: to give Christ to these children. It is grueling work, but they know the secret of the saints: persevering love stirs hearts to healing. The Sisters of Mary are considered to be one of the hardest-working congregations in the world.

Although I encountered thousands of vibrant, resurrected children at the Sisters of Mary's schools, it was the sisters themselves, these blue-collar martyrs with a redoubtable instinct to save, who shook me most. The 55 consecrated women at Chalco (there are 398 in total throughout the world) seemed like a divine paradox, spilled chalices of their Lord's Blood. They pour out their lives for their students. They die to themselves each day so devastated children can live. Every child, they know, comes from the drylands of poverty shouldering crosses heavy as the Hindenburg. Their response is to throw their arms out to bear its weight, until, like Simon of Cyrene, the cross becomes theirs as well. What was the secret to their unbreaking acceptance of immolation?

While in Mexico, I befriended cheery-eyed, Brazilian-born Sister Marinei. One night while we were speaking, I asked—in a moment of rudeness—what she had yet to die to. A curtain of awkward silence dropped between us. Barking dogs in the countryside became the only sound. Her hesitant eyes told two different stories: her self-consciousness at being caught in the teeth of a perceived weakness and, at the same time, her desire to expose it. Finally, she whispered, "I am sensitive", with the awkward smile of a kindergartner at her first picture-taking. "And I know I must give that up, too. My thoughts, my hurts—it is all nothing. I must die to everything to be filled with Christ." She went on:

> To live poverty means that I must accept a certain death. Now, it is not easy for me [she laughed], but I know I need to die several times a day. I need to leave behind everything that I am. But that is the Gospel—I leave everything—mother, father, all that I have. This is what Jesus asks. It is difficult, but these difficulties are great gifts. Because they allow me to offer myself fully to Him and these girls.

How did she attain this level of renunciation? Where did she and her religious community learn this kind of love? I began gradually to understand that Sister Marinei, like her other sisters, walks in the footsteps of Father Aloysius Schwartz (1930–1992), the order's founder. The Sisters of Mary are his spiritual daughters.

Schwartz—or Father Al, as everyone called him—formed the Sisters of Mary in 1964 in the war-scorched Korean Peninsula, with a mission to nourish the souls of the humiliated and neglected. He tended to the poor, to orphans, to lepers, to outcasts and all others on the margins. He built hospitals, schools, sanatoriums, homeless centers, houses for the disabled and for unwed mothers. The work eventually expanded to the Philippines in the 1980s. When he opened the doors to the Mexican poor in 1991, his body was fading away in the grip of amyotrophic lateral sclerosis (ALS), Lou Gehrig's disease. To Father Al, this suffering was no accident. "Our role is to mingle our blood with the blood of Christ", he once said, "and to shed our blood with that of Christ to the poor.... The way we serve is to have a constant crown of thorns."[1]

As I was writing my book *The Priests We Need to Save the Church* in 2019, I found no one—priest or layperson—like Washington, D.C.–born Father Al. In my research, I read the lives of several priestly paragons, including Damien the Leper, Vincent de Paul, John Bosco, Maximilian Kolbe, and John Vianney. Learning about Father Al's life, though, was like finding traces of a white whale on the open sea, broad and mighty and flabbergasting. Perhaps no priest in the history of the world did as much as he did for the orphaned and tormented child. "People say that Saint Vincent de Paul was the great apostle of charity and that Father Al Schwartz based his entire missionary life on his", noted Monsignor James Golasinski, who worked alongside Father Al for ten years in the Far East. "But I've told people that Monsignor Aloysius Schwartz accomplished more than Saint Vincent de Paul. What Father Al managed to do is beyond the pale. I was there, and I saw what happened."

After ordination in 1957, Schwartz raised his hand to be sent to the saddest place in the world: South Korea after the Korean War. On the Feast of the Immaculate Conception, he stepped off the train in Seoul as a fresh-faced priest and found himself in a dystopian novel. Squatters with blank stares picked through hills of garbage. Paper-fleshed orphans lay on the streets like leftover war landmines. The scene haunted him. So he reached down to lift up one child, then another. And within a few years, he had changed the course of Korean history, and many in the southern peninsula saw him as Atlas. Yet he prayed to be unknown. The reason you don't know about him is that he didn't want you to know.

Had Saint Teresa of Calcutta never come under the gaze of biographer Malcolm Muggeridge, she likely would have remained in obscurity, as Schwartz has. Mother Teresa and Father Al esteemed each other's work from afar, though their styles were different, and occasionally they crossed paths. At one of their encounters, Father Al told Mother Teresa he wanted to buy her some washing machines. The saint squinted her eyes. He explained: "Your sisters shouldn't be wasting their time hand-washing their saris. The world already

---

[1] *Serm*, 2:9, 17.

knows their humility; they should stay in the streets, working." Brash as it was, he meant it, and she understood. This was his manner, and he got away with it because he seasoned his bluntness with a wink.

"He was the boldest man I ever knew", claimed Monsignor Golasinski. "He feared nothing." By turns, Schwartz was hunted by American bishops, Korean bishops, a murderous kingpin, a gang of lepers, and his own seminary rector. And each time, he passed right through their midst. "I think he was not even afraid of God", Filipino Bishop Socrates Villegas said, "because perfect love casts out all fear.... He was only afraid of one thing. My dear children, he was only afraid of sin."[2]

But the bishop wasn't entirely right. Father Al also feared disappointing his Queen. One evening in 1957, Al Schwartz, still a young seminarian, knelt down in a countryside chapel in Banneux in weather-miserable northern Belgium. Twenty-four years earlier, the Blessed Mother had—it was said—appeared there, calling herself the Virgin of the Poor. That night in her chapel, Al consecrated his life to Mary, vowing to spend the remainder of his days surrendering his will and comforts to serve her and her poor. Thereafter, miracles came, one after the other. He would found an order in her name—the Sisters of Mary *of Banneux*—and in 1992 he would fade away while calling out her name. "I would be happy with a hole in the ground", he quipped, "and a little plaque saying something like this, 'Here lies Al Schwartz. He tried his best for Jesus.' That's it.... My apostolate is hers and I would like to be buried at her feet and say, that all praise, honor, and glory for anything good accomplished in my life goes to her and to her alone."[3]

---

[2] *Pos*, 519–20.
[3] *KMS*, 152.

I

The Littlest Commando

Washington, D.C., Great Depression, 1930–1944

LOUIS SCHWARTZ raced his secondhand sedan with balding tires past Hooverville shanties that were spreading like late-summertime mosquitoes along the southern end of Washington, D.C. After a sweltering summer of pregnancy, Cedelia told her husband the time had arrived for their third child to be born.

It would have been difficult for Aloysius Philip Schwartz to have picked a worse time to arrive at Providence Hospital than on September 18, 1930. The year of 1930 was a continuous series of landmines. The Great Depression fell like a dull axe into Washington. Abruptly cut off were opportunities for government work, and stiff Prohibition laws made it tough for laid-off federal workers to drown the creeping sense that they, too, might be pushed out of their homes and onto the vast network of D.C. alleyways. As spigots ran dry in row homes, few Washingtonians thought anymore of strolls to the Tidal Basin, to Georgetown, or even to downtown Griffith Stadium, where the beloved Senators baseball team had seen a precipitous drop in attendance. Every day, the front page of the *Washington Post* reported the latest stories of local and national heartbreak. Choking storms of dust and grit were sending farmers in the southern and Midwestern plains to their knees in the worst drought in American history. The stock market had sunk to its lowest levels ever. What started as a small run on the banks and credit unions in Tennessee and Kentucky now began to trickle northward, and before the end of the year, bankers in New York and Philadelphia were as powerless as the cropless farmers, many of whom were already en route to

California to gamble on another way of life. A young politico, Adolf Hitler, was on the rise in Europe. In sports, the darling of heavyweight boxing, American Jack Dempsey, was done, and the pride of Germany—future Luftwaffe paratrooper Max Schmeling—reigned as the king. Chicago Cubs outfielder Hack Wilson was piecing together what would become the greatest offensive display in baseball history, but few discussed this in the grim soup lines.

By the end of 1930, more than fifteen million Americans were jobless, a reality that never strayed far from Louis Schwartz's mind. His sixth-grade education was a haunting reminder that he would always be kept adrift from the firm land of the American Dream. The struggle to feed his family, which would eventually grow to nine total, was a cross to which Louis awakened in darkness daily in his narrow two-story row house at 1643 Gales Street, which stood forgettably on the outer rim of the Washington D.C. slums and on the less-envious side of Benning Road's trolley car tracks. This neighborhood in northeast D.C. was one where politicians didn't venture. It boasted an array of hard-bitten, immigrant-born, blue-collar Catholics who in 1930 began walking the streets, not too proud to beg for whatever job or sustenance might come their way. The Italians mostly kept with the Italians, the Germans with Germans, the Irish with the Irish, but everyone was cast into the same bucket; no one could escape his gut worry over the screaming economic freefall. Each personally knew of someone who'd been forced out onto the alleys.

Born in Baltimore in the late 1890s, Louis seemed to leave the birth canal into a world of nevers. He grew up in a brood of twelve children, in a poor, devout Catholic family whose origins stretched back to a tiny village near the Oder River in northeastern Germany.[1] Coagulated blood clung to the air like incense as he played stickball in the cobblestoned alleys outside his home in "Pigtown", a section of Baltimore populated with first-generation Germans who settled west of the marina. Pigtown was an oozing smorgasbord of meat-packing plants, sausage factories, and pig-slaughtering complexes. The pork was sent out to local butcher shops and markets, or carried a few blocks up the road to rail cars at the Baltimore and

---

[1] *Pos*, 537.

Ohio train station, where the meat was hauled over Maryland's rolling mountains and unloaded in western states. Louis shared ancestral brotherhood with a husky ball-playing loudmouth a few alleys away who already at seven years old drank his father's beer—George Herman Ruth, known as "Babe".

As the Schwartz family grew, Louis' father, Andrew, was forced to purchase a larger house on Cross Street a few miles away. Thereafter, he told his son that he needed to quit school; the family business needed another body for their pre-dawn prep at a cramped seafood stall in the heart of Baltimore. The family's means of livelihood was wedged within a working-class symphony of open-air butcher shops, chuck wagons, and stands selling fruit, vegetables, homemade pasta, and bread outside of hardscrabble Lexington Market, on the corner of Paca and Lexington Streets. Across the street was a small shrine honoring the oft-forgotten Saint Jude, the patron saint of hopeless cases. It is thought that twelve-year-old Louis, smelling of sweat, dried blood, and fresh-caught fish from the marina, occasionally fell to his knees in the humbly built shrine to pray for cases that may have seemed to him hopeless at the time. Long days of bucketing ice, hauling and splitting open fish, and vying for prospective buyers on busy Paca Street were punishing, but the grinding rhythm of his childhood did present one distinct silver lining—it steeled him for what was to come.

At the age of nineteen, Louis enlisted in the US Navy. Within a year, he was on the deck of a destroyer in the English Channel, where he joined a team of seamen who spent long days fishing old German mines out of British sea lanes. The work was psychologically and physically menacing; he never spoke of it upon his return to America. Much later, when his children begged him for minesweeping tales from the sea, he remained quiet, as was his custom, and cast faraway glances.

In 1926, after settling in Washington, D.C., Louis met transplant Cedelia Bourassa, a native Montanan who began to fall for her ruggedly built suitor for one reason: he was the only man who agreed to accompany her to the evening Novena of Grace to Saint Francis Xavier at the red-brick Jesuit church on the corner of North Capitol and I Street. The stately Saint Aloysius was located across the road from her job with the Government Printing Office, where she spent her days as a typist during the war years. So adept was Cedelia at her craft that the federal government had recruited her from the vast virgin plains of Plentywood, Montana, where her Canadian-born parents ran a small farm and an inn called The Grandview, near a lonely intersection of North Dakota and Saskatchewan.

In a diary recovered after her premature death from cancer in 1946, Cedelia noted that she had always held a special devotion to Saint Francis Xavier, the patron saint of foreign missionaries, and had committed herself to his Novena of Grace for twenty-one consecutive years. In the novena booklet was written, "Those who help Catholic Missionaries by their prayers and alms are carrying on the work for which St. Francis lived, suffered and died." At Saint Aloysius Church, the twenty-something Cedelia prayed for a holy husband and a happy family, asking that one day she and her future spouse might produce for the Church holy priests and nuns. She did not know that her future son Aloysius' missionary work would change the world.

The couple married at a small Catholic church in the wilds of Montana on June 27, 1927. Three years later, in September 1930, having already brought a son and a daughter into the world, Louis and Cedelia named their third child Aloysius, to memorialize the warm early days of their courtship when they spent quiet time together at the grand church in Washington.[2] They would go on to have eight children altogether, with one dying at birth.

As the years passed, Louis' hope for a decent-paying job and advancement stayed buried beneath the rubble of his status as a grade-school dropout. Although he had a firm strain of German stamina and endurance, he accepted his fate with shame. Barring God's intervention, he would never be a self-made success or secure a place in the middle class, no matter how hard he strived for it. As his hope for job substantiality foundered, he settled for a salesman's job

---

[2] It is interesting to note that the church sits on the property of the prestigious Gonzaga College High School. Aloysius would one day turn down a full scholarship offer from Gonzaga in order to start his path to religious life at St. Charles College minor seminary outside of Baltimore, along with his brother Lou. As much as Louis and Cedelia likely appreciated their son's desire to get a jump on seminary life, the scholarship refusal may have felt like a punch to the gut. The Schwartz family was poor, and free tuition to attend Gonzaga meant something. The distinction would have put their family on the map in their neighborhood, or at least would have offered it a ray of hopeful light.

at a company notorious for making lousy furniture. He knocked on doors with toil-worn hands, fell into a fake affability, and talked his way into selling couches, coffee tables, and knock-off La-Z-Boys on credit to low-income families, whom he often was forced to confront when they backslid on payments. Many of the purchasers lived near his family on the poor northeast side of D.C., which made evening strolls in the neighborhood indelicate. Coming home at night, Louis tried to empty his mind of his workday agitations. "After work, Dad spent most of the evenings napping on and off in his chair", recounted Lou Schwartz, the eldest son. "Surely he was pondering how he was going to continue to feed and clothe seven children on his meager salary. He had very little energy for meaningful discourse at that point in the night. As we headed past him for bed, we gave him a peck on his forehead as our goodnight kiss, and he'd mumble a goodnight back."

Other than a few Italian delis, a scrapyard, and a Peoples Drug Store, the Benning Road corridor where they lived didn't offer much for the eyes or for the soul. "Directly across Gales Street, we'd see families who had bigger and nicer porches. Even kids we saw seemed more pleasant than the ones on our street", Lou said. His inseparable younger brother Al particularly felt the disparity. "Al especially seemed to understand, in a quiet way, what being poor felt like. He never spoke of it. We would just walk the alleys together before school in the early morning to serve Mass at Holy Name, get to the 5 and 10 on the corner of 17th Street when we had a few quarters, and play sports as much as we could, often in the vacant lot next door. We didn't much consider our lower income level, but we knew it was there." Within this grim setting, an unseen pilot light sparked to life in little Al Schwartz. He considered becoming a priest. The flame never blinked out. "The idea of the priesthood was always with me, like a soft, warm, glow", Al wrote years later.[3]

Things turned suddenly grave for the Schwartz family in 1941 when Louis fell deathly ill. Al was an eleven-year-old in the fifth grade at Holy Name Elementary School when, one autumn evening, his father's incessant cough began disturbing his neighbors marking their bingo cards at the Saint Aloysius parish hall. He had decided to

[3] PM.

walk a mile there in poor weather, and he spent the evening in rain-drenched clothes, socks, and shoes, hoping to be the first to holler "Bingo". When his cough picked up in intensity the following day and a paralyzing weakness spread throughout his body, he learned he had developed double pneumonia. Within a week, his health had deteriorated to the point that doctors at Mount Alto Veterans Hospital didn't think Louis would live. Cedelia returned to Saint Aloysius, where she prostrated herself in grief and begged God to spare her poor husband's life. She began another Xavierian novena. Six weeks later, at the culmination of her most cherished prayer, her husband's health slowly began to eke out a recovery—though an extended and grueling one. Louis didn't set foot from the hospital for many months. "It seemed to me Dad was there for over a year", Lou said. "The fact is, I think he was."

Cedelia succumbed to resuming her old job as a typist for the government. For the better part of two years, she came home at night after work to cook, clean, and care for her children, including her last-born child, her infant Joan. Often, she stepped inside with her children already asleep in bed. Friends, fellow Holy Name parishioners, and Daughters of Charity stopped by the Schwartz home with meals and groceries. Many nights, though, oppression seemed to blanket their row home, especially on those evenings when the kids were all alone with the sounds of the night. The noise of the Benning Road trolley rumbled on through the dark, but the Schwartz family were stuck right where they were.

This period of silent sorrow is pivotal to understanding Al's formation. Between 1941 and 1942, his adolescent eyes witnessed firsthand the anguish of the human condition and the untamed desolation of poverty. The unpredictability of these days bore on Al for the remainder of his life; it was a time when God's face seemed to turn away.

Up until his dad's sickness, Al had been all boy, circling base paths as a speedy, light-hitting infielder and pulling up cages of heavy blue crabs from the South River. Al and Lou whiled away D.C.'s stifling summer afternoons at the neighborhood Rosedale swimming pool and the gargantuan playground that the brothers treated like a poor man's Disneyland. In the pre-dawn stillness, Al flung the *Washington Post* onto empty front porches of row homes and circled back dutifully in the afternoon to throw the competing *Washington Star* to men just home from work looking for the latest on the Third Reich's air raids in Britain. His job on the paper routes took up much of the day and was vital in assisting his family financially. It also provided him a pocketful of change for vanilla cones and jerky from Shulman's Market, where he would often be found walking home through the tangled alleys with an issue of the *Boy Commandos* rolled into the back pocket of his shorts.

The DC Comics sensation came in the mail periodically from his Uncle Al, who owned a five and dime store in Fargo, North Dakota, and it became little Al's multicolored secular bible. He saw the Commandos as saviors of mankind, an international cast of daring orphaned boys—Andre Chavard from France, Alfy Twidgett from England, Jan Haasan from the Netherlands, and "Brooklyn" from the United States—who together boldly took on Hitler and the Nazis. They spoke to his imagination in an intensely personal way. As he flipped pages, Al inconspicuously deposited himself into the stories as a fifth orphan, secretly joining them on another dire circumstance in "Hitlertown" and "Naziville". When the foursome yet again saved the day, Al imagined that one day he might do his part as well. And he asked himself, even then: Are priests able to save this way?

With his dad's long hospitalization, though, Al began to comprehend the full weight of his powerlessness in the face of his family's poverty, with the crushing isolation it brought. On those odd nights when neighbors or social services didn't arrive with a meal, and Mom was still working, the hungry Schwartz kids suffered in silence and unarticulated fears. They couldn't afford to escape to the movies to watch the Three Stooges, though they could have used some laughs. Reactively, Lou or Al would flick on the radio to help brighten the mood of the home. Everyone would huddle together in the small family room to listen intently to the serialized dramas—*The Lone Ranger* and *The Shadow* were favorites—but the shows sounded tinny and entirely detached from the fragility of their situation. "We were poor, and we felt poor", Lou put it bluntly. "We always got by, but when Dad got sick, some of those days became dark."

As bleak as things were for the Schwartzes, the winds of dysfunction howled stronger at the Hagars' row house next door. Lou and Al fell asleep at night in the same small bed—a thin board separated them—to the buzz saw of family disharmony they could overhear through the walls. The vitriol cut through the din of the city and coaxed neighbors to eavesdrop. The Hagar parents often screamed at each other and at their children, who railed right back. The Hagars raised bullies, and Louis Schwartz, bedridden at a faraway hospital, wasn't around to help his sons navigate past the older, bigger, and tougher boys. The neighborhood had its fill of misfits, and "Little Mouse" Al and "Big Mouse" Lou didn't have the size or stomach to put up much of a fight. Since they were altar servers, top-flight students, and—for the time being at least—without a father at home, they were easy marks. They were also confused about the proper response to bullying. While the heavily wimpled order of sisters at Holy Name drilled it into their heads to turn the other cheek and pray for their persecutors, their comic book heroes balled up their fists, even when the opponent was mightier.

"There were times I'd come home to see the oldest Hagar bully and I'd have to circle around the block a few times. They were always after Al and me", Lou reported.

> They were truly a poverty-stricken family, and they lived riotously. We ignored them the best we could. But there were other families like the Hagars; there was another up the street by Rosedale Playground. One of them, a kid named Bo, started picking on Al one day and he and I got into a fistfight. There was another family with kids up the block who also weren't wholesome. They had a kid named Porkchop. He was another bully to contend with. We spent a lot of time in real fear in those days. These were true bullies. We just had to accept it, it became a reality for Al and me.

The Boy Commandos never had to contend with such a wide radius of neighborhood toughs. Still, whenever he felt a wave of poverty, isolation, or fears rushing in upon him, "Little Mouse" Al kept reaching for his comic books. The stories always managed to warm his heart with portrayals of exceptionalism and bravery, as he searched for insights on handling the Hagars and the rest of the bunch. They ennobled him. The Commandos were true heroes, a self-sacrificing force that stepped into places no one else dared to go and saved those who had been left for dead or completely forgotten. "It was the heroes from those comic books", Lou reflected, "that got Al dreaming. They're the ones, I believe, who put him on his road."

When in 1942 Louis' health became fully restored, he returned home to furniture sales and the demands of everyday life. With a steady trickle of income starting to flow again, he was eager to set himself back in the swing of family life, and he began taking his family on day trips to make up for the lost time. On Sundays, he would load all the Schwartzes into his secondhand Nash Motors sedan, with high mileage and white-walled tires, and head off to nearby Maryland beaches or rivers or tourist spots throughout Washington and Virginia. It was at one of these destinations where providence struck and there arose an unlikely spiritual alliance between a nun and a twelve-year-old boy.

LOUIS AND THE FAMILY HEADED SOUTH late one Sunday afternoon down Benning Road, onto Kenilworth Avenue, and into the leafy hills of the all-Black community of Anacostia, where his older sister Frances (Sister Mary Melfrieda) sat on the porch of her convent at one of the highest points in town, awaiting them. "Dad's bald tires would start spinning out climbing that hill. With all of us in there, we would always struggle to even make it up that hill", Lou remembered. Sister Melfrieda was a fully habited missionary with the Sisters of Notre Dame de Namur. She used everything at her disposal—her meekness, wit, piety, and Germanic backbone—to educate her destitute Black students as a teacher at Our Lady of Perpetual Help Mission on Morris Road, which was situated a mile from the old home of abolitionist Frederick Douglass. She found contentment in the slums. There was an exact linear symmetry, she knew, between her vocation and the origin of her French-born order, which emerged in 1804 to serve the powerless, voiceless, and societally disregarded. Its first nuns were some of France's few bright lights who worked feverishly, in the same urgent manner of the great Saint John Vianney at the time, to help salvage the Catholic faith that had been garroted by the French Revolution. The Sisters of Notre Dame de Namur had always set up shop in the heart of societal darkness to offer themselves as small Alleluias of hope.

For the remainder of his life, his family's visits there would be some of his most evocative memories. Sister Melfrieda's tucked-away convent, so far away from the noise of the big city, rested like a hermitage on an isolated Siberian mountainside, Al felt. Not only did her home seem set on sacred ground, but its high elevation offered him and the Schwartz children striking panoramas of the Tidal Basin, Lincoln Memorial, Washington Monument, and other D.C. landmarks. Although all around them was a landscape of poverty, Sister Melfrieda radiated a welcome warmth and a sense of rebirth. She lived in the midst of God's most treasured souls: the poor, the disregarded, and the humiliated. She had made her schoolhouse into a humble kingdom of acceptance, and her glow and easy manner showed Al that she was entirely at home.

He had never seen anyone more enchantingly comfortable in her own skin. While his siblings gawked at the cityscape and picked from the assortment of treats Sister Melfrieda laid out for them on the sweeping front porch, Al sat listening at her feet. Her porch became the lofty balcony of a humble queen, who awoke in his heart a new world of yearning to know Christ as she knew Him. A revolution took place in Al's mind: serving the poor in the slums was not an obscenity; it was the privileged path to entering the life of Christ in the Gospels. Christ chose the poor; to work for the societally disregarded was to share in his thinking. His aunt knew this, and Al started to see the world through her eyes.

It is thought that here Al first began to understand that it would only be through an amputation of self-will that he could properly mimic Christ, the wounded King. He began to see that beautiful fruit could grow from a life of obscurity, grit, and unseen measures of charity. Sister Melfrieda's existence was rooted in a singular Christ-appointed mission: she had given her life to ennoble poor children and help them see their unique God-given dignity and value. Al wanted in. He felt an impulse to disappear like her into the slums, a fisher of men, catching the souls of the poor.

In a flash, the feats of the Nazi-destroying comic-book Commandos no longer seemed so extraordinary. As brave as those boys were, they never faced the *inglorious* heroism, the forgottenness, that Sister Melfrieda did. Hers was a stronger, purer form of nobility precisely because it took place quietly, in obscurity. She would receive no Bronze Star, no Medal of Honor. Like Jesus with the woman at the well, only the people she served knew what she had done for them.

At the same time, it became clear to Al for the first time that his own place on society's lower rungs was in line with the newborn

Prince of Peace lying vulnerably in a crude animal stall, unnoticed by all save some lowly shepherds. When, in accordance with Levitical Law, Jesus' parents presented their first-born son at the Temple in Jerusalem, their poverty reduced them to offering two turtle doves—the option for Jews who could not afford a lamb. Later, Joseph chose the forgotten backwater of Nazareth for the Holy Family's home, and this did little for their status. ("Can anything good come out of Nazareth?" derided the apostle Nathaniel, when he found out Jesus' hometown.[4]) Al began to grasp that the King wore a royal cashmere robe of forgottenness. His aunt explained to him that the Savior was marginalized, poor, and bullied, just like him, and just like the Black children peeking out at them from the narrow lanes of the neighborhood that surrounded the convent. As Al's heart was being lifted there on the porch, Sister Melfrieda looked at her nephew and understood that in him were the makings of someone special. From that day forward, she began to pray for his vocation.

Even before that first rendezvous with his aunt, Al showed indications that he wanted to dedicate himself to Christ. He told his siblings, some cousins, and a few select friends that the priesthood intrigued him. One evening at a Schwartz holiday dinner with the extended Baltimore family—his father's side of the family, whom Al treasured for their boisterousness and blue-collar-charmed personality—Al shared that he wanted to become pope. Riotous laughter filled the room, and Al sat quietly and smiled. They didn't know he meant it. Although family and friends could see an uncommon goodness in him, few took his inspirations seriously.

Before his school days began at Holy Name, Al joined Lou for mile-and-a-half walks in darkness to serve weekday Mass for the Irish priests at Holy Name. Though his altar service sprang partly from a sense of duty, there was, we can imagine, also a hidden mystical dimension. Lou agreed. "I have to say that serving Mass for us may have just been *pro forma*. It was for me", he said. "With Al, you just didn't know. He didn't share in that way." Yet Al's relationship to the Mass transformed after his first visit to his aunt. "Something in him changed," explained Lou, "and things weren't *pro forma* any longer. It was in [Sister Melfrieda's] presence that Al slowly began to

[4]John 1:46.

understand God's plan. He wanted to be among the poor, and he wanted to serve them as Christ did. But the big thing is that I think it was the beginning of his understanding that he had to be poor to care for the poor."

Al began to beg his father for return trips to his aunt's convent in Anacostia, where the good sister continued to groom him with little tales of her care for the children who surrounded her schoolhouse. As his siblings devoured Sister Melfrieda's endless dishes of treats and frolicked in the spacious acreage that spread out around the convent, Al and his aunt were becoming linked with a deep spiritual bond.

THEN ONE DAY, something unexpected happened, as if a secret room in his conscience were suddenly entered for the first time. He began to believe that Sister Melfrieda and the Sisters of Notre Dame de Namur lived too comfortably. "Life inside the convent seemed different from the real world outside", Al recalled later. "Everything was so immaculately clean, cool, quiet, and comfortable. Even the cold drinks and sweets the nuns gave us tasted different and so much better than what we were accustomed to at home."[5] A suspicion began to rise within him. The Sisters' care for the poor seemed to him to be "phony". When their days concluded, they returned to a world of relative comfort, whereas the Blacks they served and taught came home—just like Al's own parents—to "a day-in, day-out struggle to make ends meet", as he put it.[6]

Where once Al saw the romance of his aunt having renounced the world to serve a people who had largely been renounced by society, he wondered whether the Sisters of Notre Dame de Namur were really living Christ's call to "sell what you possess and give to the poor ... and come, follow me" (Mt 16:21). He dearly loved his aunt and knew she had given her life for another race of people. He also recognized that the Sisters "could not be considered rich". But he knew, too, that Jesus lived as a poor man, not like the Sisters of Notre Dame. The incongruity of it all rattled him.

By autumn, Sister Melfrieda was gone. His aunt was needed as superior at the all-Black Saint Augustine School in Buffalo, New York.

[5] PM.
[6] PM.

But the mysterious undercurrents of the Holy Spirit were in motion, and an unshakable conviction emerged in him: to serve the poor, one must become vulnerable; one must, himself, be poor. "I guess this is why I felt more attracted to the secular priesthood as opposed to the religious life", he later explained in his journal. "I felt that it offered an existence that was somehow more authentic and more real."[7] His aunt was rarely seen by the rest of the Schwartzes again, but she would keep up correspondence with Al for the rest of her life. Included in her obituary from September 1959 are these words:

> Her heart went out to her colored charges, and she gave them the full measure of her devoted love. Sister Mary Melfrieda was a real apostle. She saw Christ in the dusky face of every colored child she taught and tried to make him realize his dignity as a child of God and a member of the Mystical Body. Every lesson she taught was impregnated with this one idea: Her little pupils did not have much in the way of worldly possessions, but she wanted to make sure that they would be spiritually rich.

Father Al's obit thirty-three years later would read remarkably the same.

In the days and months that followed his trips to Sister Melfrieda's, Al asked to tag along with his mother when she volunteered to serve the Black communities near their home. During this time, as there budded in him an earnest longing to renounce worldly things, he launched into the practice of small penances and mortifications, forgoing sweets and snacks and taking on unnoticed chores around the house. He set up a small chapel in an unused space in the basement, where he began to spend long periods in prayer. By the time he was twelve, he had begun to mimic the rubrics of the Mass. He kept this closely guarded, but nevertheless found himself embarrassed one evening when Lou walked in on him in the middle of "celebrating" the Holy Sacrifice of the Mass.

The comic-book Commandos he used to fall asleep to at night were now pushed aside by a storehouse of martyrs, saints, prophets, and lonesome missionaries he dug up in borrowed, dog-eared books.

---

[7] He also added, "I subsequently discovered that one can be just as much a phony as a secular priest or as a member of a religious congregation." PM.

Their lives lit fires in his soul. And just like that, Superman gave way to Blessed Charles de Foucauld, and the mysterious Lone Ranger became the mystic John of the Cross; Captain Marvel couldn't rescue poor kids the way John Bosco could. These sacred new heroes opened for him a vast and deep desire to live like Jesus Christ. As he read the lives of the saints, he saw that many resembled Christ as a starved man, one whose face was beaten and whose body was stained with blood as he gave his life for all—the poor, the rich, and even the riotous Hagars next door. These saints, Al saw, wanted to succor Jesus by offering to him a reflection of his own life; they wanted to serve, suffer, and die as he had. It was during these days that Al first began to stretch his mind to consider what it would take to become someone who, like his aunt, offered his life to destitute families suffering indignities, families not dissimilar to his own. Those closest to Al saw small, charming changes taking shape within him, but no one could have grasped his deepest intentions. He kept his dream of becoming a missionary priest in another land close to his heart.

In the eighth grade, the secret of his spirituality was opened up to his teacher, Sister Theophane, along with his Holy Name classmates. Al won an essay contest with a piece titled "My Desire to Become a Priest". Then in the springtime, when his classmates argued for the zoo and a local amusement park as the final two choices for a field trip destination, Al raised his hand to say they might want to consider the Franciscan monastery up the road, which boasted a replica of the Roman catacombs. He got his wish. Shortly after the Holy Name class disembarked on the trip, a classmate of Al's recalled, some boys started to mock the destination, but Al stepped into the dissension and redirected things. He was no nerd, and he had the respect of everyone.

"He just had that way. He was liked and admired, wherever and whatever the situation", Lou said. "The Sisters at Holy Name singled him out. He studied hard, he played sports hard, and he laughed hard. He had something special, the fruit of which was pure, and that was the key. But the whisperings of the Holy Spirit were just that— whisperings inside him. They were deeply personal. I didn't know, no one really knew, where he wanted to take things."

2

Seminary Traps

St. Charles College and Maryknoll Formation, 1944–1952

NOT A SOUL was caught by surprise when Al followed his older brother Lou to St. Charles College High School, a large diocesan preparatory seminary located in Catonsville, a leafy suburb on the western edge of Baltimore, Maryland. In the fall of 1944, though, there was already a cavernous gulf separating the Schwartz brothers. Lou was entirely unsettled on his vocation or even on what he wanted out of life, while Al was set on becoming a missionary. Even as a fourteen-year-old boy, young Al was already considering martyrdom. Although the Sulpician priests who staffed the seminary worked to raise "pious young men ... for the ministry of the gospel", just 11 of the 121 in Al's class would eventually be ordained.

So intent was Al on safeguarding the missionary blueprints his aunt had inked indelibly into his mind that before committing to St. Charles, he demanded assurances from the Sulpician rector that his zeal for working on the peripheries would remain unthwarted. Father George Gleason wasn't accustomed to such pluck from incoming students, but he assured Al that his ambition would remain faithfully supported. Within no time, though, the teenager suspected that this promise would not be kept, and he would constantly have to be on guard to keep his missionary inclinations alive. "I liked St. Charles'. It was a good place to begin the long road to the priesthood", Al wrote not long after being ordained. "It was not, however, a good place to keep alive the spark of a missionary vocation."[1] Still, he

---

[1] *StSi*, 15.

remained quiet and at peace. Al had already understood from the saints how spiritual battles are won. Like Francis de Sales and Patrick, he would push on despite countervailing forces. He would pray his way through.

One memorable evening at St. Charles, a gladiatorial Maryknoll priest of Irish bloodlines, Father Patrick Byrne, came into town like a cassocked John Wayne on horseback. Father Byrne had a masculine magnetism, instantly recognizable to a teenage boy. With a gift for storytelling that boasted everything except a lilting brogue, he gave an auditorium full of seminarians rousing and heartfelt accounts of the front line of missionary life. The jolted teenagers fell noiseless as a spirit of heroism filled the space. It was the most seductive call to action Al had ever heard. Byrne threw out the alarmingly persuasive challenge to consider spreading the one, true Catholic faith in post-war Japan, whose heart had been torn open by the loss of more than a quarter-million citizens in the atomic bombings of Hiroshima and Nagasaki. Japan's soul had been stolen, Father Byrne told them, and its survivors were searching for a new way. That new way, the priest continued, involved the sacramental energy that they, as young St. Charles seminarians, had the power to bring. *They* could be the balm of Japan, just like Saint Francis Xavier, whose life Al had absorbed from the pages of a book in his bedroom on Gales Street. Byrne said that as future anointed priests of God, they would carry the cure in their own hands. Al was floating that night; he could hardly sleep. "[Father Byrne's] enthusiasm and fervor were contagious", he later wrote. "That night many a young seminarian went to bed dreaming of faraway places with strange-sounding names."[2]

Father Byrne, who was at that point one of St. Charles' most distinguished alumni, had turned legend before the age of forty. He traveled to the Far East nine years after his ordination in 1915, where he worked tirelessly and successfully to establish Maryknoll's first mission in Korea. Within no time, a large population of Catholics and seminarians began to spread across the Korean countryside. Seeing the mission flourish, Father Byrne departed for Kyoto, Japan, to proclaim the gospel to a population mostly unwilling to receive it—but experienced enormous success there as well. So powerful was

---

[2] *StSi*, 16.

Father Byrne at winning Catholic converts in the Far East that Pope Pius XII named him a titular bishop and the first apostolic delegate to Korea.

Six years after his electrifying talk at St. Charles, in the brutal heat of the summer of 1950, Bishop Byrne's valorous spreading of Catholicism would catch up with him. He gained the attention of North Korean Communists, who imprisoned and tortured him. He was ordered by a North Korean judge to condemn the United States government for threatening to aid the South Koreans in their brewing tensions, and to condemn the Vatican as well. Byrne is said to have replied, "There remains only one course: that I die."[3] Communist soldiers marched Bishop Byrne and hundreds of other POWs across what became a blood-stained landscape in the shadow of Korea's snow-covered Kangnam Mountains. In the middle of winter, and with virtually no food, water, or warm clothing, many dozens of prisoners died en route. Byrne, who made the 110-mile journey in a pair of thin slacks and a short-sleeved shirt, frequently stopped to pray with those who crumpled in the snow and were left to die. When after four months he staggered with a few dozen other survivors into the North Korean town of Hanjang-ni, he was asked to perform calisthenics in subzero temperatures. He died shortly thereafter of pneumonia. It is reported that just before his death on November 25, 1950, he said to his fellow POWs, "After the privilege of my priesthood, the greatest privilege of my life is to suffer for Christ with all of you."[4]

It is no surprise, then, that Father Byrne had the strength and charisma to inspire the boys at St. Charles that night. But he couldn't have known how quickly his appeal would be deflected.

The day after his departure, the Sulpicians—with whip-like speed—initiated what Al saw as a missionary devitalization effort. "The rector of the seminary was very upset by Father Byrne's success", Al later recounted in his book *The Starved and the Silent*, "and the very next evening he delivered a counterattack in the form of a long talk stressing the need for local diocesan vocations." A week later, Baltimore's chancery office dispatched one of its priests to underscore

---

[3] Eileen Ryan, "Marching to Martyrdom in Korea", *Maryknoll Magazine*, July 1, 2017.
[4] Ibid.

the importance of working toward a vocation in their own backyard, and even "hinted that those who sought out other pastures were somehow disloyal to the home diocese", Al remembered. "Father Byrne and the missions didn't have a chance." He would note this as a much broader phenomenon in the contemporary Church:

> Although all the recent popes have strongly urged bishops to encourage foreign mission vocations in their diocese, most bishops are too concerned with their own local needs to make more than token efforts in this direction. Often, not only do they not encourage vocations to the field afar, but they actively discourage them. One mission vocation director whom I know refers contemptuously to this attitude on the part of certain bishops and seminary superiors as "spiritual birth control."[5]

Al regarded the tag-team of the Sulpicians and the chancery office as a well-organized canceling-out of a potential movement of transcendence. This awareness, however, only intensified his desire to become a Father Byrne–like figure in a foreign land; one day, if God winked at him, he might even get the chance to minister right alongside the visiting missionary priest.

"It was a boldness that lived in him", said his old friend Monsignor James Golasinski. "His boldness was so unusual because it defined everything he did. And he was never taken down, because he was a good priest with the truth and goodness on his side. He took things on, walked straight into them, and dealt with whatever came.... What kind of man knows at the age of fourteen that he's going to be a missionary? Only a bold man knows that type of thing."

Father Al would later write in his journals:

> The objections [of formators] run something like this: "Why run off to Korea or India or Africa when there is such a need for vocations right here at home? The south and the southwest, the rural areas and the slums of every big city are literally crying out for dedicated missionaries." ... [But] one of the most baffling paradoxes of Christianity is that in order to fully realize one's capacity as a child of God, one must surrender freely and joyfully all that he is and has in an interior act of abandon.

---

[5] StSi, 16.

Christ invites one to lose his life in order to find it; He says that one must renounce home, family and material possessions if one desires the fullness of grace; one must even abandon his will, desires, and care for the future in order to live from day to day in search of the Kingdom of God which is within one. This total renunciation of self is the only door that leads to fulfillment of self.[6]

With his missionary zeal unsupported by the Sulpicians, he nonchalantly gravitated to football, baseball, basketball, and track, where his speed and diminutive stature enabled him quick bursts past defenders in whatever sport he played. He was slowed down when he broke his leg in a football game and spent a large portion of his sophomore year walking the large campus with crutches and a cast. He sat at a lunch table with his best friends Terry O'Brien, Jack Seipp, and future semi-pro pitcher Andy Dietrich. The foursome discussed all manner of sports, especially the Washington Senators and in particular Al's favorite player, All-Star first baseman Mickey Vernon. Although these topics held sway at their table over philosophy, English literature, and Latin classes, they couldn't quite displace the faith, not for Al. When discussions at the lunch table centered on Christ, the discipline of prayer, and the possibilities of service within the Church, Al's facial expression took on a stillness and quiet resolve that made an impression on his friends. "Al was an excellent athlete, good at football, baseball, and basketball", Jack Seipp later wrote in a letter. "He was very well-liked as a person and very smart in the classroom. He had his head on straight. Even from the beginning as a freshman, when entering the chapel, Al had a certain reverence about him; you might say as if he was talking to God."[7] Al's friends knew he wanted to live truly for Christ. Still, he kept his thoughts close to his heart. He knew he was different. Often, he slipped undetected into a far corner of St. Charles' library to read missionary adventures from the latest Maryknoll-published *Field Afar* magazine.

Still, Al and his friends didn't quite walk the straight and narrow path in those early years at the minor seminary. Too often he

[6] PM.
[7] PM.

watched his classmates fall asleep at Holy Hour without being nudged awake by priests. Whereas Sister Melfrieda had introduced him to spiritual warfare, self-denial, and devoted prayer, he saw complacency at St. Charles, and he began to feel a spiritual malaise and boredom overtake him. He filled the void as most effervescent teen-age boys did: with dorm room pranks. "There were some unhealthy divisions and too much hazing between the different classes at that time", Lou explained, "and although Al knew he couldn't be a part of that type of dissension, he was still a boy with a lot of energy." Teasing and bullying were practically a tradition at St. Charles. "As a first-year student," said Lou, "Al was a 'Crusto', and I was a second-year 'Termite.' I'll never forget how bad I felt at not protecting my little brother when the Termites went after him one day with those terrible 'pink bellies'."

But "Little Mouse" gave as well as he received. For all his piety, Al became entangled one day in a since-forgotten transgression, and he was summoned into the office of Headmaster Father Joseph White. It was the custom then at St. Charles that misbehaving seminarians were spanked with a wooden sandal. Father White, renowned and respected for his Greek, Latin, and English instruction as much as for his form of discipline, was said to have used his sandal at one point or another on every one of the students. The unwritten rule was to spank the offender with as many strokes as was necessary to bring about tears. The school record was fifty-two; Al made it to thirty-five.[8]

Lou contends that Al, who left Father White's office in silence and shame, was never the same after the incident. "He didn't share it with anyone, but that spanking, in a healthy way, had a profound effect on him. It seemed to awaken him to some things he was straying from. He was humbled. He suddenly seemed to become more serious about what he had signed up for.... This was when, I believe, he began to see that he needed to let the Holy Spirit fully into his life. He knew if he was to be a missionary, the Holy Spirit had to lead him." Indeed, Al himself would write about that day as a pivotal moment: "After leaving Joe White's room, I limped downstairs to the chapel, knelt before the Blessed Sacrament, and said simply,

[8] FA, 26.

'Thank you, Lord, I needed that.' After that, I became more serious and more mature concerning seminary life."[9]

Shortly after his visit with Father White, someone thought to give young Al Saint Thérèse of Lisieux's autobiography, *The Story of a Soul*. Thereafter, everything changed. He was struck by her "little way" of renunciation. The French saint, with her impulse to embrace hiddenness and the dignity of suffering, with her faithful perseverance in offering unnoticed acts of sacrifice, with her desire for total abandonment to serve God, captivated him as no other saint had. Even as a sixteen-year-old, he saw that "the substance of [her] writings [is] inspired with the fire of the Spirit and the blood of the Lamb", as he wrote in his private journal. He would later request of his longtime spiritual director in Korea, Belgian Carmelite nun Mother Gertrude, that she pray fervently that "Thérèse herself puts into my heart, my bloodstream, and the very marrow of my bones what is contained in that book."[10] Over the course of his life, he would go on to read *The Story of a Soul* more than two dozen times—often in Thérèse's original French—and made it mandatory reading for each of the Sisters of Mary nuns. As he was dying from ALS, one of his final requests was that the Little Flower's deathbed conversations with her Carmelite sisters be read aloud to him.

AL GRADUATED from high school in 1948 as one of St. Charles' top students and was accepted as a candidate into the Maryknoll Society, where he joined other aspiring missionary students pursuing their bachelor's degrees at Maryknoll Junior College in Lakewood, New Jersey. His striving for selflessness and his comfort in his own skin made an impression on his classmates and formators. He was voted president of his class and served as editor of the school magazine. He distinguished himself not only as an athlete but as a thinker. It seemed he was another red-blooded "Jack Armstrong", like many good Maryknolls before him. To be labeled a Jack Armstrong—taken

[9] PM. More than fifty years later, when Father Al was in the throes of death, an aged Father White would write to Al's sister, Dolores Vita, "I feel sure that time will put [your brother] among the best of the saints. I feel he is among them now." Father White had followed Father Al's missionary work from afar. He continued, "[Al] went so far beyond what charity could demand or even request that I feel utterly ashamed. He is a Mother Teresa."

[10] *Pos*, 375.

from the radio show of the same name—was to be an all-American "everyboy", dutifully pouring himself a bowl of Wheaties each morning before throwing the winning touchdown pass for his school later that night. Al couldn't stand the label. But Al distinguished himself even more through his fervor and his deep prayer. He hungered for the uncompromising life of a mendicant.

Early in his formation, he sensed that, for all its virtues, there was something tinny, bourgeois, and even defective about the Maryknoll Society. He liked his classmates and instructors, the dogmatic and doctrinal framework was sound, and overall, there reigned a spirit of "hospitality, simplicity, warmth, and joy". But he had gradually come to see that many of the Maryknolls, like many other American missionaries, lacked a real inner struggle with poverty, still more a longing to embrace it. It seemed that the missionaries would often camp luxuriously *outside of* poverty-stricken neighborhoods. Al not only wanted to live with the poor; he wanted to *be* like them. He felt that until the walls of physical and emotional comfort were annihilated, false gods would always live in missionaries' bellies, and the souls of the poor would never be wholly fed.

Al couldn't help noticing how some of the overseas missionary houses provided hot showers, three square meals, a radio or TV, modern plumbing and furnishings, and even a mirror or two on the walls. He regarded such a setup as a scandal to the impoverished. Ever since the first seed of foreign missionary work was planted in him, he had imagined his days lived in poverty as he served and catechized the ignorant and the abandoned, returning alone in the evenings to withdraw into a small dwelling to read Scripture, pray his Office, and contemplate Jesus Christ as a poor Man. The Maryknolls and their heavily Americanized missionary style left him disillusioned.

"Maryknoll was closer to Jack Armstrong and the all-American boy type than to Francis Xavier or Paul of Tarsus", Al would write in *The Starved and the Silent*. "What I discovered was this: Maryknoll was rich; unmistakably so. Considering that these students are preparing themselves for an apostolate to the poverty-stricken peoples of Asia, Africa, and Latin America, who are at the opposite end of the economic spectrum, one cannot help wondering if this arrangement is not something less than the ideal. That one should prepare for a life among the poor by living rich struck me as being at least a bit illogical."[11]

In 1949, shortly after transferring to Maryknoll's brand new seminary in Glen Ellyn, Illinois, to continue his studies, he doubted he could commit his priesthood to them. Put simply: he wanted to be poor, which he feared they would never be. Only the poor and fully sacrificial priest, answering Christ's call to give up all, would radiate a lasting, unfiltered light. "The life at Maryknoll was too rich, comfortable, and luxurious. There was not enough thrust and zeal for the poor", he shared in a sermon years later to a group of Sisters of Mary nuns. "I looked at this style of life and looked at the poor overseas to whom we were going. There was something lacking there. There was something contradictory, which made me unhappy."[12]

Yet finding no good alternatives, Al kept his feelings hidden and pressed on in his formation: "I resigned myself to remain with Maryknoll—certainly not the worst fate which could befall a young man aspiring to the missionary priesthood."[13] On summer breaks from seminary, he caught the bus back to Washington, D.C., where he joined his family at their new home on 11 Channing Street. It was a row house slightly larger than their old one across town. Although he could spot the Capitol dome from the roof of the new house, Al spent the majority of his time at home in the basement, where he went to sleep at night by a pile of coal that warmed the Schwartz home in the winter. In the summer months, his unventilated underground bedroom was dreary and stuffy and carried a substantial musty odor; what's more, he had to share his living quarters with rodents. It bore no comfort, and this is exactly as he wanted it. Saint Thérèse of Lisieux had resolved to offer every humdrum moment of her life to God as a miniature holocaust of love, and Al tried to follow her brilliant design. She had made her life into a game of inches, offering herself as a sacrifice to God unnumbered times throughout the day, even in the smallest details. Al began to offer the scuffling noises of the rats and mice, the incessant pounding of siblings' footsteps above, and the stifling conditions of his bedroom as a renunciation of self and

[11] *StSi*, 18.
[12] *Serm*, 1:143.
[13] *StSi*, 19–20.

sacrifice to God for souls. In time, he began to see that his unseen penances were acting as small springboards to the sanctification of his life. He learned from Thérèse, who he claimed "was more mighty oak than little flower",[14] that the rejection of self was the sole method of rising like incense to God. He knew her little way of self-denial would help to secure the safe passage of his priesthood; he would just ignore the best he was able his issues with the Maryknolls.

At home in D.C., Al befriended Mr. Kelly, a house painter who lived a few houses away on Channing Street. Being in the painter's orbit meant breathing in the unmistakable scent of alcohol that he had consumed the night before. Al made a vow to Mr. Kelly—if he promised to teach him how to paint in a professional manner, he would do whatever he could to help make his small business a success. Together, the unlikely pair began to answer ads in newspapers, where they grabbed up any job they could lay their hands on: picket fences, interior walls, new coatings on backyard sheds, or maybe even the entire exterior of a house. Often, Mr. Kelly didn't have it in him to rise from bed in the morning, so Al spent the day in Washington's summer humidity painting alone. "It was like a dance to see if Mr. Kelly would work that day. Al would show up around five A.M. and walk into Mr. Kelly's house to wake him up", Lou said. "They formed a small friendship this way. Al sure needed the money, but the truth is, my brother was trying to convert Mr. Kelly. He worked with him each day to help him get his life back together." Al knew it wasn't another pint of liquor that Mr. Kelly needed—it was the feeling of being wanted.

Upon his return home from a long day of painting, Al ate dinner and conversed with his family, then retreated to the sanctum of his basement catacomb, where he remained committed to steadfast prayer, the reading of Scripture, and the mock celebration of the Mass—which he usually practiced while bathed in sweat. "Summers in D.C. were unbearably hot and humid, but Al seemed to relish the work", remembered Al's sister Margaret Mercier. "I can still picture his brawny arms with hard-working muscles and smiling face speckled with paint at the end of each day. [Mr. Kelly] wanted Al to abandon school and his plans to become a priest to assist him on a full-time basis. This became quite the joke in the family."[15]

[14] PM.
[15] PM.

The grueling job was his way of throwing himself into poverty. "There are no two ways about it," Al would later write, "'poor man' poverty—such as Christ lived—is painful.... Christianity is the religion of the Incarnation. As such, it always deals with man, not as an abstraction, but as the concrete flesh and blood reality which he is."[16]

By his fourth year of formation in Glen Ellyn, Al had become bored with the Maryknolls—an order he now knew he would need to abandon. More and more, the missionary proclamations, the calls to "hear the cry of the poor", rang in his ears as pious-sounding rhetoric. He had formed close friendships with his brethren and valued their desire to serve, but he felt strongly that if their service lacked the trial and desolation of the Cross, of real solidarity with the poor and suffering, it would be hollow and ineffectual.

Al wanted to paint with the palette of the great paragons—Anthony of the Desert, Patrick cold and tethered to an Irish mountainside, Benedict in a cave, Francis of Assisi alone in a crumbling chapel in a forest. His impulse was to oblige a radical form of poverty, separation, and amputation of will. He felt uniquely called to suffer like Christ, who writhed with agony on the Cross and had no place to lay his head, who surrendered his will entirely to his Father through total denial of himself. "Christ himself was marked by the sign of poverty", Al observed in his 1970 book *Poverty: Sign of Our Times*. "He was born under it, lived under it, died under it. If not, we could end this discussion of poverty right here. The fact is, however, the historical Christ chose to be poor and a concomitant fact is, his disciples have no choice but to follow in his footsteps."[17]

Although what he saw as an Americanized sterilization of missionary life caused Al enormous distress, he continued to thrive within the system. He was among the top students in his class, and Maryknoll administrators were bending his future away from the mission field and toward the classroom or administrative desk. This recognition is what finally convinced him to leave the Maryknolls definitively.

HE HAD BEEN LOOKING for other American orders with a more austere charism—"three things: the missions, the secular priesthood, and

[16] *Pov*, 58, 67.
[17] *Pov*, 17.

a mystique of Christian poverty"[18]—but kept coming up empty. The Maryknolls were the kings of the hill. He eventually broadened his search overseas, where he discovered an obscure and small group of priests known as the Société des Auxiliaires des Missions (abbreviation SAM, or the Samists), whose home base was located in a little country town outside of Louvain, Belgium. The Samists proposed what they termed "a new mission formula", forming secular priests who would work with and under native bishops in Africa and Asia. The Samists required its community of priests to embrace fully the identity of the people they served. They wanted priests speaking the local people's dialect, eating their same food, wearing their same threadbare clothing, and embracing their customs, poverty, and humble ways. Their work, Al saw, involved abandoning one's self to live entirely on the fringes of society—a prospect he deemed romantic, rugged, and most importantly, in line with what had been distinctly mandated to him by God.

He had finally found a home where he could continue his theological studies. He had struck gold. *This* was priestly holiness, he thought. He wrote to the Samists' superior on June 6, 1952, "S.A.M. seems to be 'the' missionary work of the 20th century and at present, it attracts me very strongly." After his impressive resume and top-flight grades were reviewed, Al was accepted. He was the first seminarian in the history of the Maryknoll Society to leave to join another group overseas.

Yet when he informed his family at the age of twenty-two that he was leaving both the Maryknolls and America, it seemed a bomb had been dropped. Not a single person—not even Sister Melfrieda—thought he should flee from the Maryknolls' conventional, time-tested missionary structure. They were blunt in urging Al to remain on the course he had been following for years. He recalled the scene in a sermon he gave to a gathering of the Sisters of Mary in 1989:

> Everybody was convinced that I had lost my reason—everyone. I recall my aunt, a very holy nun [Sister Melfrieda], who was very devoted to me and was living for the day of my ordination. It was announced that I was going overseas and she wrote me a letter. I got

---

[18] *StSi*, 19.

it the day I was leaving. She said, 'You are making the biggest blunder of your life.' She was so upset. She was considered the Solomon in our family, the wise old nun. This was her advice. I had a cousin who was a Dominican and I saw him the day I was getting on the boat. He told me I was stupid. My brother told me I was stupid. Nobody encouraged me.... This was the atmosphere in which I left and went to Louvain.[19]

Shortly after Christmas of 1952, he began finalizing his plans to move to the Catholic University of Louvain, where he would begin to acclimate himself with members of the Société des Auxiliaires des Missions—a group of priests no one knew, with a name no one could pronounce. He asked his eldest sister, Mary, who at the time was in formation to become a Daughter of Mary in Emmitsburg, Maryland, if she would finance his trip. She gave him every penny of the $150 she had been saving for the chalice she wanted to present to him on the day of his ordination. As Mary recounted, "He said if he could not get to Belgium, then he would not need the chalice."[20]

A few weeks later, Al boarded a ship for Europe.

[19] *Serm*, 1:145–46.
[20] PM.

3

Arrival and Departures

Entrance into the Société des Auxiliaires des Missions, 1953–1957

WHEN AL UNPACKED his small suitcase in his shoebox-sized bedroom in Louvain on January 7, 1953, he was already four months behind in the semester course load. There was, however, an even more pressing issue: only French and Latin were spoken by instructors in class. French he didn't know, and outside of the Mass, he had never paid much mind to Latin. He quickly began working day and night to catch up, burrowing himself in the library, the chapel, and the ice box of his sleeping quarters. He was forced to warm his body each night with heated bricks that gradually chilled as the frigid nighttime hours pushed on.

"I would put on long underwear and socks, heat a brick on the coal stove in the room, wrap that in a towel, putting it at the bottom of a sleeping bag and then crawl in, zip it up, pull the hood over my head, and hope to be warm for the night", he wrote in his journal. "The other 20 or so European seminarians were born in that cold, damp, inhospitable climate of Northern Europe and seemed to thrive on it. I could understand how such a climate killed St. Thérèse of Lisieux at the age of 24."[1]

He would later share with his family that his first semester in Louvain, Belgium, marked the most psychologically and physically grueling period of his life. He had arrived at a time when the country was still reeling from the devastation of World War II. He could see that many of the Belgians were heavy-hearted and solemn. A bleakness

[1] PM.

seemed to blanket the small farming community of Kessel-Lo, where his dormitory was located. "I was starry-eyed ... and off I went into the wild blue yonder", Al would later put it. "Only it wasn't blue: it was gray and leaden."[2]

Even as he worked to master French and Latin and make up for missed class time, Al, the lone American seminarian, was regarded by some Samists as a nonconformist—a Yankee missionary wannabe who'd ditched the Maryknolls because he considered their order too soft and his own constitution too tough and holy. He was the odd man out, and he felt it. But he hunkered down and did what he could to dismantle the cowboy tag. As a general rule, Al made it a point to stay quiet and bestow unspoken measures of kindness upon each person he encountered. All the while, he was persevering in his classes. He not only caught up to his classmates, but then began to pass them by.

Happily for Al, his theology instructor his first semester was Canon Gustave Thils, who at the time was one of Europe's most esteemed Catholic thinkers. The Belgian-born theologian had just published his *Théologie des réalités terrestres* [Theology of Earthly Realities], a comprehensive study that sought to address the Christian sway on social, political, technical, and artistic realities throughout Europe. The priest's work became widely discussed and won a large European audience. Eventually, he would also make key contributions to the Second Vatican Council.

It is thought that Thils took an instant liking to the American seminarian for his daring, lone-wolf approach in moving to Louvain blindly from the States. Thils became not only Al's friend, but his spiritual director, which gave him a closer look at the Washingtonian's interiority, with its well-worn grooves of thought on missionary life. Al's spirituality had a twist, though, to which Thils wasn't accustomed. Not only did the young seminarian not fear the desolation brought on by the trial of the cross—he *wanted* it.

Al cheerfully told Thils he wanted to suffer peaceably as a "poor-man priest", emancipated from every worldly comfort, because identification with the mortified Christ was the surest sign of him in the world. This was the narrow road blazed by the first apostles. If a

---

[2] *StSi*, 20.

silent and hidden martyrdom wasn't part of his work, Al seemed to say, then to hell with it. A missionary life void of a certain type of death would inevitably have disastrous consequences. It can be imagined that Thils, an intellectual whose writings had placed him in the spotlight of a large stage, sat quietly marveling at the seminarian. His directee was intent on becoming a saint, Thils knew, and Al was not the type to take shortcuts.

That first semester, Thils awarded the Société des Auxiliaires des Missions' only American seminarian the grade of a high B in his dogmatic theology class, just a few months after the transplant had begun to learn French from scratch. High grades would once again characterize Al's time in seminary. But although top marks came easily, he never gained a comfortable footing in Belgium. Persistently miserable weather—apparently the norm in the university town—disturbed his long forty-five-minute walks and bike rides from the tiny village of Kessel-Lo to his classes in Louvain. His socks, shoes, and pant cuffs seemed to be always water-logged. Illnesses and a mysterious stomach affliction marked the early months of his first semester, the beginnings of a digestive condition that would plague him for the remainder of his life. Because the seminary food often made him ill, Al ate sparingly, which contributed to the thinning of his already slender frame. Few students ever addressed him in English, and he dearly missed home. But the inconveniences, maladies, and lonesomeness were part of the dying process he had requested from God.

During this period he began to plead with God, in a particular way, to allow him to suffer the same indignities of Christ's crucifixion. When years later he spoke from his wheelchair prior to his death from ALS, he pointed back to this particular time in Belgium, with a bit of self-deprecation. Throughout his priesthood, in the brutality of his work and the seemingly excessive demands of God, Father Al's journals would reveal a charming light-heartedness in his descriptions:

> In my early twenties, I prayed or contemplated in a very romantic, sentimental, idealistic manner of encountering great suffering, sickness or a trial. [I imagined] if I were to come through this, I would come out purified and perfected. I longed for this and I prayed for this. If I realized that ALS was the answer to my prayers, I doubt I would have continued in this vein. But, somehow, this seems to be exactly what

was in my imagination or my prayers over forty years ago. Is this the
workings of extrasensory perception or a mystical experience of grace
or both? I think it's both. But, at any rate, years ago I thought I was
being prepared for this terrible ordeal.[3]

Little by little, as the winter finally ceded to the springtime thaw,
Al managed to establish some friendships within the Samist community. And by the time explosions of cardinal-red poppies began to fill
Louvain's valleys, most of the community had come to esteem the
invigorating spirit of the cheery American, whom they now regarded
as a welcome asset with an unshakable loyalty to the Samists. Al came
across as easygoing, mannered, and simply a fun guy to be around.
No one within the Samist community heard him complain about his
digestive issues, his string of illnesses, his disrupted sleep in his frigid
room, or even how much he missed his homeland. In the meantime,
he worked relentlessly at tearing down the language barrier. But even
with the communication difficulties, his classmates enjoyed being
around him for his joy and his humor, often at his own expense; he
frequently could be found smiling and laughing around campus. And
he was establishing a reputation for his intellect and his devotion.
The Samists knew Canon Thils didn't waste his time whiling away
afternoons with weak seminarians.

When summer arrived, Al was too poor to return home, and his
family was too poor to buy him a ticket. As a reward for surviving
his taxing first semester, he launched out on a hitchhiking trip through
the heart of France, with his course set for a small mountainside parish in southeastern France. The village of Bauduen was dropped like
the tiniest of pebbles in the wild countryside of the Provence-Alpes-
Côte d'Azur in southeastern France. The aging priest Abbé Duggot
had sent out a bulletin requesting the assistance of a seminarian to
help with parish duties and lend a hand in the village. A deal was
struck: if Al agreed to work alongside the locals as a steady farmhand,
he would receive free accommodations, healthy country fare, a pleasant mountainous climate, and the opportunity to improve his French
in a pastoral setting.

Al's summer in Bauduen turned out to be one of the most memorable of his life, mostly because of the time he spent in the shadow of

[3] *KMS*, 151.

a priest he regarded as holy and wise. Illness had forced Abbé Duggot into parish work after he'd spent twenty-five years in a French
Trappist monastery. To Al, he seemed still an alpine monk and mystic, praying and celebrating a beautiful Mass in his small chapel each
day. Al and the curé shared strong devotions to Mary and prayed
the Rosary together nightly in his poor mountainside rectory. They
were both deeply drawn to the life of the French saint John Vianney,
the Curé of Ars. Villagers throughout the mountainous region also
revered the holy witness of Abbé Duggot, whom they considered a
miracle worker. He healed the afflictions of hard-working farmers
with his hands.

Al wrote of Abbé Duggot in a letter to his family:

[Abbé Duggot] asked the bishop for the loneliest and most difficult
post in [his diocese] and he was sent here. The house is very poor; no
running water (there is a pump around the corner of the house); no
toilet (a hole in the ground suffices), no icebox, no radio, washing
machine, iron, or any conveniences. We have meat about once or
twice a week; we eat very simply, but very, very well—plenty of fresh
vegetables and fresh fruit and cheese and bread which the parishioners
very quickly leave on the doorstep of the rectory.

The Curé is deeply loved by the people. He has a terrific reputation as a chiropractor and people come from miles for his help. [On
Saturday] when we went down into town in his 1934 rattletrap which
the bishop gave him, he healed three different men. I was amazed.
One [man] had a sprained back and could hardly walk but after the
Curé worked on it for five minutes, he jumped up and down and was
fit as a fiddle. Another had a sprained leg and walked away from the
Curé without limping or without pain. The good sister thinks he is a
miracle-worker but she has a rich imagination. At any rate, however,
he certainly has a wonderful gift.

What am I doing to keep out of mischief? Mostly painting,
masonry work, [time] in the garden, and going along with the Curé
on his rounds.

In letters he sent home later that summer, Al described how he
had managed to develop friendships with people in the community
of 250 villagers by working alongside them each day. "All [here] are
farmers, goat herders, or shepherds. The village dates back to the
Romans and is the most picturesque [town] I have ever laid eyes on."

He wrote once, in charming detail, of a shepherd who invited him to join him as he tended to his sheep on a hillside:

We didn't return until 10:30 at night; the impression was wonderful—completely alone in the valley with the sheep and the dog and watching the stars come out. It was so marvelously easy to relive the drama which took place on the hillside in Palestine when Christ was born.

One thing about the life here: it gives a real understanding of the life of Christ, which was lived in a country of farmers and shepherds and in a climate very, very warm like that of this part of France.

Al wrote of the bronzing of his skin while spending hot afternoons "breaking the dry, cracked earth with our picks in search of potatoes—real back-breaking labor." He also told of his many bee stings while helping Abbé Duggot collect honey from his prized hives. "We've had a wonderful harvest—about 200 pounds of honey!"

He also related a humorous story of wanting to present himself admirably to the young women of the village:

This past week I've been collecting nuts (don't laugh, I'm serious). [Abbé Duggot] has about six almond trees parked inside of a neighboring mountain, and every day I go gather a burlap sack full. It's really great sport; you have a long pole, stand under a tree and start beating the branches. It's like standing out in the open during a heavy hail storm—for the almonds pour down for a full 20 minutes.

Yesterday I returned with a 30 lb. sack of almonds; the fruit of only two small trees! Something funny happened yesterday on returning. I took [Abbé Duggot's] bike to go yesterday and tied the 30 lb. sack on the back of the bike. All the young maidens of the village were at the square when I was returning. I really felt proud of myself in my peasant outfit, all dirty and sweaty with my harvest. As I passed, I gave them my biggest and most innocent smile and a "Bonjour mademoiselles!", which of course they returned. Then all of a sudden, a big crash—as my 30 lb. sack slipped off my bicycle.... I felt the eye of every young maiden of Bouduen on my sweaty countenance. Boy, did that take the wind out of my sails![4]

Al returned to Louvain in the Fall healthier in spirit and body, invigorated, and eager to resume classes. By Christmas, he had proven

[4] PM.

himself to be as excellent a priestly candidate as any the Samists had. He was one of his seminary class' strongest students and completed the 1953–1954 semesters with high honors. All indications were that he was on his way to becoming the first American ever to complete formation with the Samists. In the summer of 1954, he celebrated the completion of a successful school year by setting off on another hitchhiking trip, this time destined for the south of Italy.

As a testament to Al's degree of trust that God had a watchfulness over him, he departed for the thirty-day sojourn with little more than a winning smile and twenty-five dollars (ultimately returning to Louvain with six left in his pocket). He chronicled each day of his road trip in an eighteen-page letter he sent to his father at the end of the summer, reporting at one point, "[I have allowed] myself a dollar a day in expenses; I can do it if I play it right, choose my food with a housewife's sense of economy, and never pay for a place to stay." Al departed Louvain as the second passenger of a priest friend's motorcycle. In his backpack were a few of his devotional books, a Bible, a change of clothes, a thin sleeping bag, a rosary, and little else. After saying his goodbyes to the priest at a prearranged point of departure, Al hung his thumb for the southbound country roads that would take him to Italy's southernmost tip. He instantly encountered a pair of high-spirited Scottish teens who were hitchhiking in their kilts. His first night on the road was spent beneath a blanket of stars on a pleasant night at the base of a mountain in Luxembourg. He wrote to his father, "I find a very thick pine woods, unroll my sleeping bag on the soft pine needles, crawl in, and sleep like a baby until six o'clock when the sun peeks its head over the pine-covered, rolling mountains."

It can be imagined that Louis wept, as proud fathers often do, when reading Al's letter and realizing that his son was experiencing life in a manner he never could. Clearly evident in the travel log was the young man's ability to make friends with complete strangers. (Some individuals he met on this trip later wrote to him, and one even tracked him down years later in Korea.) He simply connected with folks. Unpretentious, he bore no artificialities; you got what you got with the cassocked, wide-smiling seminarian.

His travels took him through Austria, Germany, France, and Switzerland, where he slept in barns, thirty-cent hostels, rectories, monasteries, on beaches, in villagers' homes, in an Italian orphanage, in a railway station, and even in a four-star hotel. The latter was paid for by an American State Department official visiting Rome, who insisted on buying Al dinner and filling his suitcase with snacks and candy. Al hunted down an early-morning Mass wherever he went, dined primarily on bread, cheese, tomatoes, and fruit, and often walked through villages, visiting and praying in their chapels, and passing the time getting to know the locals.

It was on this trip that he developed a confidence that God would always provide for him, whether it was a place to sleep, a loaf of bread, or an encounter with a particular soul. He just went where he thought God wanted him to. He kept a travelogue throughout. Below are some typical entries, describing six successive travel days:

Friday, August 20—Spend another leisurely day strolling through town [in Italy], talking with the monks. The monks want to make a little Franciscan out of me, and their efforts at propaganda are really comical. They are goodhearted and I like them. Feed me good.

In half an hour I get a ride by a truck driver 250 miles across Italy to Bari on the Adriatic Coast. Beautiful ride, beautiful day and it feels good to be moving again. Get a place to sleep in a Franciscan monastery.

Saturday, August 21—Visit the town [Bari] a little. Two beautiful 10th-century Roman cathedrals. Hot as blazes. Get a couple of rides for about 50 miles. Just too hot and the beach on the Adriatic Sea only 100 yards away. Too much to resist! ... Go for a nice swim in the Adriatic Sea. [Spend] the afternoon on the beach and cool off.

Go to sleep on the beach, listening to the music of the waves and looking up at the stars.

Sunday, August 22—Wake up at about 5 o'clock, wash, get my gear together and walk about one mile to the nearest church for the 6 o'clock Mass. Beautiful Roman Cathedral which dates from the 12th or 13th century. After Mass, I walk to the main highway, make a sign to the first car that comes along. He stops and takes me over 500 miles to the north, as far as Florence. What luck! Driver is a very nice, young Italian engineer. Follow the coast road for a while, then cut across to Naples, then up to Rome. He had a couple hours of business in Rome. So he lets me off and promises to pick me up at 6 o'clock. I get a big bowl of hot spaghetti and a bottle of wine to wash it down.

Make a visit to St. Mary's Basilica. At 6 o'clock sharp my "chauffeur" picks me up and on to Florence. The road is bad and as we pull into Florence, the tower clock is striking 2 o'clock in the morning. Too late to find a place to stay so I go to the railroad station to sit around until morning.

Monday, August 23—Meet a German boy who gives me the address of a monastery which offers room to boarders. Sounds good. At 7 o'clock I am knocking at the door of the monastery, and in half an hour's time I am in a soft bed soundly sleeping off the fatigue of the day's journey. Wake up about 12 noon, completely refreshed. Spend the remainder of the day visiting the town and its art treasures.

Tuesday, August 24—After Mass and breakfast, on the open road once again practicing my much-loved but humble profession of hitchhiker. Well, what do you know! Meet my two Dutch friends whom I had met down in Sicily. Also meet a nice English boy who is heading back to England. Get my first ride by a very nice German couple to the next city which is Bologna, heavily communist so they say. Get my next ride by an Italian cancer specialist who is very, very nice. Decided to stop here in Modena for the night. Ask an Italian gentleman who I see in a church if he can direct me to a seminary or a college where I can find a place to sleep. Without a moment's hesitation, he invited me to his house. I eat supper with his family and get a nice room. Wonderful people!

Wednesday, August 25—A few short rides until about 11 o'clock. Huge flat and gentle plain of Lombardy—between the Alps and the Apennines, [the] Po River cuts it in two, grape vines and apple orchards.

At 11 o'clock, I strike it rich once again in my own inimitable fashion. An American officer and his British wife pick me up. They are going to Germany and I ride all day with them. Rainstorms in the mountains. [They bought] me a wonderful dinner. We kid and joke all day. In the afternoon we cross the Italian Alps into Austria. Lovely green mountainous country. About 7 o'clock that night we come into Innsbruck, a lovely resort town. Since they are going north to Germany and I wish to go west to Salzburg, we separate. They insist on giving me all their Austrian money (about $3) and invite me to their place in Germany for 2 or 3 days when I am free. In five minutes I have a nice room with the Austrian Redemptorist Fathers. Guess I just live right![5]

5 PM.

After returning to seminary for the fall semester at the age of twenty-five, Al had discovered the unconventional work of a long-bearded, beret-wearing French priest named Abbé Pierre (born Henri Groués), a former World War II resistance fighter who founded what came to be known throughout Europe as the Emmaus Movement. The priest's widely known mission gave the poor, homeless, and refugees of World War II a place of accommodation, somewhere to eat, and—perhaps most uniquely—a steady place to earn a living. His efforts were regarded as groundbreaking at the time because he managed to find work for people seen as the dregs of society. He surmised that homeless men and women would regain their dignity through their labor and begin to reconnect with society. One unintended effect was that in feeling the euphoria of Lazarus from the grave, many returned to God and the full practice of their faith.

But it wasn't until Abbé Pierre's speech on Radio Luxembourg on February 1, 1954—an impassioned call that begged the French people and government to come to the aid of the homeless during an especially brutal winter—that the Emmaus community found its footing. Staggeringly, the priest's radio plea generated several million dollars in donations almost overnight. It was reported that the national postal service couldn't handle the deluge. One French newspaper wrote that an "uprising of kindness" had been sprung in France. An excerpt from Abbé Pierre's speech should be noted:

My friends, help ... A woman froze to death tonight at 3 A.M., on the sidewalk of Sebastopol Boulevard, clutching the paper that, just the day before, had evicted her from her home ...

Each night, there are more than two thousand who wither under the cold, without food, without bread, a few almost naked. In the face of such horror, the *cités d'urgence* [lodgings for the homeless] are no longer urgent enough!

Listen to me: In the last three hours, two aid centers have been created: one under a tent at the foot of the Panthéon, on the Rue de la Montagne Sainte-Geneviève; the other in Courbevoie. They are already overflowing; we must open them everywhere. This very night, in every town in France, in every quarter of Paris, we must hang out placards beneath a light in the dark, at the door of places where we have ready blankets, bunks, soup; where, under the title "Fraternal Aid Center", one can read these simple words: "You who suffer, whoever you are, enter, sleep, eat, recover hope; here you are loved."

The weather forecast is for a month of terrible freezing. Faced with their brothers dying in poverty, all men—for as long as the winter lasts, for as long as these centers exist—must be of one will: the will to make it impossible that this continue. I beg you, let us love one another enough to do this right away. May all this sorrow bring forth for us something wonderful: the shared soul of France.[6]

The French priest's speech and the windfall of donations for the poor were the talk of the Samists. Hopeful to get a firsthand look at the community of workers, Al took to the road again over winter break, bound for Paris. Hitchhiking, he arrived at the Emmaus house on a moonless Christmas Eve. As Al stood outside the door in a sleeting rain, a whiskey-voiced man beckoned him into a large kitchen warmed by more gruff-talking men, hot food, and a well-tended fireplace. Al's mud-caked cassock dragged across the floor as he headed for a table, where a bowl of soup, greasy potatoes, a hunk of cheese, and a glass of "vicious-tasting red table wine" were set before him. It was there where he would go on to celebrate the most memorable Christmas season of his life.

At a solemn midnight Mass in the community's small, candlelit chapel, Al found a seat on a backless bench next to Maurice, who "had one of those hard leathery, ageless faces which could have been 55 or 35". The Frenchman was a murderer and an ex-convict who had recently been forced to Paris' streets because no employer would take him on as a bricklayer after his release from prison.

Also at Mass was Jean, a once-suicidal laborer who had been living beneath a bridge on the Seine. Filbert, Marcel, Robert, Sheriff, Monsieur St. Vincent, Guillaume, and other hard-luck men had also gathered for this Mass that may have seemed to the celebrant more like a fireside chat among the dregs of Paris. Al, though, didn't see it that way. "I was convinced that the 'Divin Enfant' who had not come to call the Pharisees or the just felt quite at home in this milieu." The incense of the Mass got lost in the scent of sweat and a sawdust-burning stove, but to Al the fragrance was sacred and ambrosial. Like the shepherds descending the Bethlehem hillsides, the coarse men in

---

[6] "L'appel de l'Abbé Pierre, du 1 février 1954", Fondation Abbé Pierre, https://www.fondation-abbe-pierre.fr/la-fondation-abbe-pierre/la-vie-de-labbe-pierre/appel-abbe-pierre-1er-fevrier-1954 (translated by Ignatius Press).

his midst—once gnawed by loneliness, rejection, and the cold of the night—came just as they were, and offered just themselves.

After Mass, Al acted as the servant for the most rollicking Christmas party he had ever attended. "A more boisterous, undisciplined, but likeable group I had rarely laid eyes on", he wrote. "They sang, danced, and told jokes, and the men pounded the tables, clapped their hands, and whistled until they were red in the face." He continued:

One young Frenchman called an older Italian worker a "macaroni". The Italian refused to accept the injury. The two were standing there glowering at each other, fists clenched and nostrils breathing fire. I was waiting for the ignition when Jean Yves, the director of the community, walked over, picked up a pitcher of water and smilingly poured it over the head of the Frenchman. The refectory rolled with laughter as the Frenchman meekly sat down in the ashes of humiliation.

The party lasted until seven in the morning. I walked over to the barracks, climbed into my bunk, and fell into a dreamless sleep.

He spent all Twelve Days of Christmas—and then some—working construction in the bitter cold alongside the robust Parisian homeless, "the toughest of the tough ... former Legionnaires, ex-convicts, soldiers of fortune, clochards (vagrants) and victims of unhappy circumstances who had been caught up in the mechanism of an impersonal society before finally being cast off as waste products". He came to regard the men as the most fascinating people he had ever known. Each morning in the dark, Al joined three hundred of his bunkmates in the bracing weather for work projects at various locations. He described the experience this way:

We were lurching and rumbling over dark country roads with their half-frozen human cargo. The work was hard—digging foundations, pushing wheelbarrows of cement, carrying cement blocks. To make matters worse, the winter rains had transformed what should have been firm ground into knee-deep mud.

After supper, we talked a little, but by 8 o'clock nearly everyone was in bed where it was warm. To my surprise I noticed that the men were much more content during the week when they were working than on Saturday and Sunday when they were loafing. The therapy of hard work was used with much success in this community.

I had grown fond of these men with their blunt, open ways and rough-hewn humility, and it was hard to say goodbye.[7]

As Al entered into the hidden mystery of the poor in Abbé Pierre's Emmaus community, he felt the same burning within as the pair of disciples on the Emmaus road in the Gospel of Luke (24:13–35). So moved was Al by the camaraderie with the men that he returned the following summer, where he blended with the Emmaus ragpickers scattered throughout the city.

Later that same summer break, he hitchhiked to serve alongside Franciscan missionaries in the blazing heat of the Moroccan desert, where a small monastery outside Marrakesh had been established to honor one of his heroes, the martyr Blessed Charles de Foucauld. At this late stage in his seminary formation, the figure of de Foucauld— who had lived quietly, lovingly, and austerely among the Tuareg people in southern Algeria, speaking their language and living their customs, the sole Catholic presence in that land—brought his soul to a crescendo. Foucauld saw it as his mission "to look upon every human being as a beloved brother", even when conversion was not possible.[8] Al, too, wanted to preach Christ in the wilderness, even if no one cared to listen to a word he had to say. He wanted to feel the abject poverty of loneliness, deprived of all worldly consolations yet full of an inexplicable joy. This was the way of de Foucauld, who once wrote, "I no longer want a monastery which is too secure. I want a small monastery, like the house of a poor workman who is not sure if tomorrow he will find work and bread, who with all his being shares the suffering of the world."[9] Al traveled many miles to lay hold of this spirit, and the words of Father de Foucauld played like a record in his soul as he returned to Louvain for his final year of seminary in 1956.

He couldn't have known the turn his life was about to take. After thirteen years of seminary formation in three different states and on two different continents, his superior wanted to take it all away.

---

[7] PM.

[8] Quoted in Jean-Jacques Antier, *Charles de Foucauld*, trans. Julia Shirek Smith (San Francisco: Ignatius Press, 1999), 325.

[9] *Charles de Foucauld: Writings*, ed. Robert Ellsberg (Maryknoll, NY: Orbis Books, 1999), 9.

4

The Problem

A Crisis in Al's Vocation, May–June 1957

IT WAS MAY 29, 1957, and all around was open sea. Al stood alone on the uneven wooden deck of the *S.S. Maaschem*; the humble ocean liner was all he could afford to take him back to America. At a lonely point in the Atlantic Ocean, he began to read a book of Father Vincent Lebbe's letters from the Chinese mission field, and as he turned the pages, a switchblade seemed to flick open in his soul. He was pierced. Lebbe spoke to him as few others could.

It is thought that after Al set down the book, he descended into the bowels of the German-built ship to write to the superior general of the Samists, Father Dieudonné Bourguignon, a man who had come to have a distaste for him. And no matter how many times Al tried to shake it, the thought of Father Bourguignon produced ripples of dark memory in his mind. The letter Al was about to write him, on fire with Lebbe's words, would prove to be a misstep, one that would change the course of Schwartz's life.

To understand the inferno in his heart there on the *S.S. Maaschem*, one should know of the holy Belgian priest who helped to set it aflame: Vincent Lebbe. "Lebbe stories" had been passed around the seminary for years like cups of sugar from one neighbor to another. During his time at what would later be renamed the Vincent Lebbe Center at Catholic University in Louvain, Al had heard dozens of tales of the missionary's exploits. There wasn't a single seminarian who didn't hold up Lebbe as a sort of Wild West hero. To Al, the stories were sacred heirlooms.

Born in 1877, a missionary to China, Frédéric-Vincent Lebbe had a barrel chest and a thick horseshoe mustache that flared out when he shook with laughter, which was often. He shaved his head bald, and although he possessed what seemed a deep interior peace, he had a silent fierceness in his gaze that spoke of something untamed. He had a set of eyes that made folks take a step back. After he mastered the native Chinese language, Mandarin seemed to roll off his tongue with swagger and grace. He was uncompromising in proclaiming the gospel; he feared nothing and no one. His love for Christ and his willingness to offer his life for the Chinese people garnered the respect of a wide assortment of the population. He journeyed deep into mountain ranges to soothe the souls of Catholic peasants, terrified of another Boxer Rebellion. But he also managed to win over pagan Communist generals and the Chinese soldiers he eventually served alongside in the Battle of Rehe against the Japanese. While Lebbe tended to the war-wounded, soldiers began to refer to him as the "old fighter". They once watched the Belgian priest race up to a Japanese bomb and kick it out of harm's way.[1]

Al saw in Lebbe an embodiment of a missionary life both temporally aware and deeply spiritual, a crossbreed between the old soldier Ignatius of Loyola and the contemplative John of the Cross. To Al, Lebbe was part revolutionary fighter, part mystic, unafraid of being hanged for proclaiming Christ precisely because his priesthood had become inflamed by prayer. He was the gutsy champion of the oppressed Catholics hiding in the hills—and the American seminarian set his sights on becoming just like him.

As Lebbe catechized the Chinese people, he began to see that peasants hungered for native-born bishops to shepherd them. Only when the Chinese saw the witness of *their own* clergy's blood spilled in the face of the Communist system—not just the sacrifices of European missionaries who didn't speak, act, or look like them—would Catholicism root itself in the land and begin to spread throughout China. Fellow missionaries told Lebbe a native-born hierarchy was an impossibility, but Lebbe was intractable in his fight for the Chinese people. He began to lobby the Vatican and started a long crusade for an indigenized Chinese hierarchy. After some time, as was his custom, Lebbe got his way. It is due to the Belgian missionary that the first six Chinese bishops were installed by Pope Pius XI in 1926.

---

[1] Jacques Leclercq, *Thunder in the Distance* (London: Sheed & Ward, 1958), 279.

He hadn't set out to be a reformer, however, when he first departed Belgium for the Far East on a cold winter day in 1901. He'd gone simply to proclaim the gospel and die for God. He arrived at a time in history when martyrdom was likely. When his ship docked on the Chinese mainland, thirty thousand Chinese Catholic peasants, many dozens of priests, and countless Christian missionaries had just been massacred in the Boxer Rebellion, an anti-Christian revolution whose embers were still being stamped out. For Lebbe, though, dying for God was just part of the job; martyrdom had been percolating in his mind since he was an eleven-year-old boy.

His uncommon desire to die for Christ came to the surface one summer day when he and his mother, Louise, were visiting a convent in the Flemish countryside village of Ypres. "Freddy", as he was called then, was reading, gripped by a book on the life of then-Blessed Jean-Gabriel Perboyre, a nineteenth-century Vincentian martyr who would be canonized by Pope John Paul II. Young Lebbe became riveted by the events preceding Perboyre's death, which bore a striking resemblance to the Passion of Christ. Perboyre, too, was sold by a disciple for silver, stripped of his garments, dragged to various tribunals, beaten, tortured, then hung and strangled to death on a cross. At some point that afternoon, Lebbe set the book down and approached his mother, who had been sharing a leisurely conversation with a nun. "I am going to be a Vincentian and go to China to be martyred", Lebbe said. Right then, aware of her son's rare constitution, Louise accepted it as his fate.[2]

Lebbe had been raised at the close of the nineteenth century in a warm and devout Catholic home in the Belgian countryside. His parents encouraged their children to have independence of thought as long as it didn't stray from the bounds of virtue and the Magisterium. Lebbe's father, Firmin, a public notary who had once owned a saloon, attended Mass each morning and made the Stations of the Cross in the afternoon. Louise, it is said, had whimsy and a good-heartedness that charmed Freddy's friends. Though the Lebbes' finances were meager, what they did have was spent mostly on their children's education. Freddy gravitated toward writing, art, and theatre in school, where he was never reluctant to share what was on his

---

[2] Leclercq, *Thunder*, 18.

mind—and often, it was Christ. Early on, he said he wanted to be a great saint. He set his course by bending his innate cheerfulness into hardy ascetical practices. He swam at a local outdoor pool until late autumn to toughen himself. And, after reading a book about Saint Gerard Majella, he began to follow the saint's example of licking the sign of the cross on the ground. He wore a spiked iron belt on many days. He managed all this with ease, and often with a smile.

Years later, while crossing the Red Sea on the way to enter China for the first time, Father Lebbe changed his name to Lei-Ming-Yuan, to unite with a people he didn't yet know but already loved. Translated, the name meant "the thunder that sings in the distance".[3] Within a short period, tens of thousands throughout mainland China would know the name. After his ordination in Beijing as a Vincentian (or Lazarist) priest, he became a giant, igniting one of the most widespread and prodigious Catholic missionary efforts in centuries. The spread of Catholicism throughout China in the early part of the twentieth century was due largely to the work of Lebbe, who adopted Chinese dress, manners, appearance, and thought as his own. He presented to the Chinese an alternative to the brutal, godless life of Communism; they could enter with him into the tender crucifixion of identifying with Christ as a Roman Catholic. Most he met chose Christ.

When Lebbe landed in China in 1901, he was clear-minded about the rigors of converting souls to the pilgrim faith. He bore no patience for fellow missionaries who sought lifestyles that didn't reflect the Savior whom they had vowed to imitate. Each disciple, Lebbe thought, should fall asleep not knowing if the next day might lead to his martyrdom. Fellow priests, Lazarist missionaries, and even the new Chinese Catholics he had led to conversion began to see his zeal for Christ as something primordial, something resembling the apostles of the early Church. Before long, most around him held him in awe.

Al Schwartz was a ten-year-old boy when Lebbe was captured by Chinese Communists and tortured in 1940. His captors attempted brainwashing, which was an often successful tactic used to break the Christian spirit. But they got nowhere with Lebbe, whom after

[3] Leclercq, *Thunder*, 37.

weeks of abuse they threw onto the streets, halfway dead. His kidneys and liver soon failed, which caused his skin to yellow and his stomach to balloon. As he lay dying in a hospital bed in Chongqing in June 1940, squadrons of Japanese planes were dropping bombs outside his window. At the time of his death, loved ones believed Lebbe looked more Chinese than Belgian. It is said his final words to the priests that surrounded his bed were, "If [my suffering] isn't enough to make saints of you, I'll suffer still more."[4] Aloysius Schwartz would return to these words throughout his priesthood.

The Chinese government flew flags at half-mast in the days following Lebbe's death. It was a secular bow to honor a man's will to give all for God and for the Chinese. By the time of Lebbe's passing, twenty-six native bishops had been ordained, and Lebbe had helped to lead countless individuals to conversion. He accomplished all he had set out to do. With the pilgrim faith now secured in China, missionaries like Al Schwartz could begin to train their eyes on Africa, South America, and other untapped lands.

WRITING TO HIS SUPERIOR in the narrow cabin of the working-class ocean liner, Al undoubtedly had the bold, candid Lebbe on his mind. He had been splitting his time on the voyage "scrupulously" rehearsing the rubrics of the Mass and reading a collection of Lebbe's letters.[5] Not only was the Belgian missionary, who had been left for dead on a Chinese street two decades earlier, a missionary exemplar to Al, but in fact the work of Lebbe had helped launch the Samists into existence. Al had understood with the SAM that a missionary priesthood necessitated a certain kind of death, and Lebbe showed him how to carry it out. Sacrifice demands *becoming* the poor that you serve.

As Lebbe gambled all for the Chinese people, Al determined he would gamble with the words he addressed to Father Bourguignon, whom all of Louvain knew as "Bou". Though Al began the letter with trepidation and vulnerability, in moderately broken French, his tone swiftly changed course. His words may have seemed to its recipient as unanticipated rounds of artillery fire.

[4] Leclercq, *Thunder*, 318.
[5] *Pos*, 320.

Dear Father,

I write these lines with trembling hands as I had often when I came
to your office to talk with you. But the same frankness and naivety
that characterized my visits with you for two years, I now open
my interiority....

You have cruelly abused the confidences that I gave you.... My
health suffered much from it. You will say that I was sick before, but
believe me, Father, it was one [to] 100; the same sickness perhaps
but a hundred times aggravated; it is for this that I did not tell you
anything before leaving Louvain. I told myself to wait for the moment
when I am well rested and completely patched up; after a week at sea,
I am sufficiently rested to calmly and objectively judge.

You arrogantly and proudly treated the reflections which I presented to you [at our meetings] .... You told me that we foreigners
are *jealous* of the fact that S.A.M. is in Belgium. That we only have to
adopt ourselves ... if we were not satisfied with the actual situation,
we had to go ... and the Flemish, they only had to integrate into
the community.... I think that it is possible that your words in a *rare*
moment of anger surpassed your thought, but you did not say anything later to correct your words.

I do not wish you to preach on the occasion of my first mass.... I
do not like to hurt you, Father, but I am obliged to follow my con-
victions. I am convinced of the fact that to invite a Belgian superior
to preach at the first mass of the first American Samist is to declare to
America that S.A.M. is a truly international Society. That is hypocrisy.
I am thinking of asking my cousin of the Dominican order to give
the homily. Excuse me if I hurt you.... But to go to the end of my
thought, you asked me for my advice regarding your visit to Washington. I never showed enthusiasm about it and now I request you to
squarely abandon it.

I think that your presence will give a false impression, i.e., that
S.A.M. has an international spirit. Moreover, my family is composed
of simple people. They will not understand how a society so poor as
S.A.M. can pay for trips that are so expensive.[6]

The letter, driven by the zeal and guilelessness of youth, was startling. Indeed, it seems misbegotten, if not rash. It can be imagined
that when Father Bourguignon read it in his office back in Belgium,
he began to blanch by the third paragraph. Perhaps he was already

[6] *Pos*, 317.

beginning to form a plan. He was a man who had gained renown for his intransigence, whose soul had been terribly rattled by hostilities he endured as a prisoner of German concentration camps. Upon his eventual return to Belgium, he was a different person. "He came back from there angry. His temper was famous", Father Golasinski said. "And everyone knew about it."

Aloysius Schwartz had picked a fight with the wrong man, but he believed that justice demanded he do so. As he progressed through the seminary in Louvain, he noted that a wall of provincialism had been built into the fabric of the Samist community. Whenever a position of authority or administrative responsibility was awarded to a seminarian, it habitually went to a French-speaking Belgian member of the community. Al and a coterie of other foreign-born seminarians were left feeling stranded by the system. It was a Belgian monopoly. It snubbed any insight or perspective from those outside of the club. And they knew "Bou" was behind it all.

Dieudonné Bourguignon was born and raised in the French-speaking village of Theux in northwestern Belgium. Like Al, he wanted to be a saint at an early age. While Bou was a student, SAM formators saw in him a budding willingness to suffer and die for Christ. He blended all the natural virtues: cleverness with humility, verve with obedience, and fearlessness with quiet piety. Following his ordination in 1936, Bou was sent to universities throughout Europe to promote SAM vocations and offer invitations to consider the missionary life. His eloquence proved compelling to young men, some of whom eventually set out to join him.

At the beginning of World War II a few years later, Bou was asked to join an underground resistance movement to do what he could to slow the spread of Hitler's Nazism. After finding success in helping Jews to go into hiding in Verviers, Belgium, he became a prominent member in the *Front de l'Indépendance*, a group that provided intelligence to the Allies; all the while he intensified his work of saving Jews. The task was remarkably dangerous, but he persisted until he was eventually discovered by German soldiers in 1943. He was imprisoned and shipped to four separate concentration camps—Esterwegen, Essen, Gross-Strehlitz, and Dachau—where in his desolation he did all in his power as a priest to console skeletonized prisoners. After escaping death by way of a mysterious technicality, Bou staggered back to the safety of Belgium and the SAM community. Although his physical health was eventually restored, a post-traumatic volatility had entered him. The camps transformed him and haunted him; whenever a seminarian, priest, or layman came into his presence, he couldn't be certain which Bou would emerge. He achieved ignoble notoriety for his stubbornness and explosiveness. Every seminarian—all clergy in Louvain, in fact—had either experienced firsthand or heard stories about Bou's brawling temper.

For better or worse, Al received the distinction of being nominated by his peers as "Senior Student to the Superior". In other words, he was handpicked to be the seminarians' mouthpiece, sharing with Bou the students' day-to-day gripes and concerns—perhaps the Arctic-like condition of the chapel, the thin coffee, stale croissants, or the severe-grading mystical theology professor. Although Al accepted his role, he was under no illusions about the choppy water into which he was wading. He knew who he was. His blunt sincerity was likely going to set in motion Bou's wrath. Still, with a sense of duty, Al held firm to articulating what his seminarian brethren had brought to him, no matter who it was standing in front of him.

After some careful sparring, Bou considered some of the seminary minutiae, and concessions here and there were made. Inevitably, though, when the conversation advanced to the Belgian monopoly, things spiraled acrimoniously. Al surely spoke with blunt-force candor, and it is thought that Al told Bou that the climate he had established within the community was one Lebbe would have abhorred. He had essentially made Belgians the favored race, and all others hoping for a say or a position of authority were left voiceless. The system lacked charity, an international spirit; and to a certain degree it was mocking to their sensibilities. According to Monsignor Golasinski, after Al finished his complaint, Bou all but picked Al up and threw him out into the dampness of the dormitory.

As the semester pushed into the dreariness of the Belgian winter, it became clear to Al that Bou was not going to be persuaded to give even an inch. Al accepted his powerlessness and backed off. In their meetings thereafter, he stuck with the less thorny issues. And why not? He was, after all, just months away from being ordained a Catholic priest.

Al's gesture of peace came too late. His relationship with Bou had been irreparably damaged, and a shadow of annoyance seemed to overcome the superior general whenever Al came into his presence. Noting Bou's mood, Al pivoted to the practice of everyday piety and readying himself for the demands of a priesthood of poverty. Part of that movement included an implementation of ascetical practices— days of fasting, sleeping on the floor, praying Rosaries with arms extended, an intensified prayer life—helping him grow closer to Jesus Christ the Starved Man.

In the *Positio super vita* for Father Aloysius Schwartz—the collection of documents, witness interviews, and personal writings compiled by Vatican investigators in order to declare him a Servant of God—the letter to Father Bourguignon, written on the boat ride to America, is introduced rather benignly: "Al Schwartz's letter saying that he did not want his superior to attend his ordination."[7] But in truth, that aspect was just one of the forty-one sentences that leaped like flames from Al's letter to his superior. The letter revealed that over time Al had grown disillusioned and even permanently repulsed by the cantankerous manner of Father Bourguignon, a man scarred by war, whose thick scabs covered long unhealed wounds that Al, with his sharp words, had just torn wide open.

Al's closest Samist friend, Father Étienne de Guchteneer, was awaiting Al in a rental car when he disembarked on a hot early June morning at a New York harbor. "Guch"—who would soon depart for his missionary assignment in Japan—steered his car south toward Washington, D.C., where Al was overwhelmed at the sight of his family, who hadn't laid eyes on him in more than four years. Tears, laughter, and a Prodigal-Son-like feast marked the day. Even though they wouldn't have him for long, "Little Mouse" had finally made it home, and the Schwartz family rarely had been happier.

At the end of the month, he was to be ordained. Thereafter, he would take off for South Korea to, at last, begin his long-sought work. The box of ordination Mass cards had just arrived at the Schwartz house from the printers, and on the front was the face of a man none of them had ever seen before. It was Father Vincent Lebbe.

ON JUNE 12, 1957, less than twenty-four hours after reading Al's letter, Father Bourguignon wrote in quick succession both to Al and

[7] *Pos*, 317.

to Washington Archbishop Patrick O'Boyle, who was set to ordain Al in seventeen days. His letter to the bishop, in uneven English, lays out some apparently disturbing details about Schwartz's mental health:

Your Excellency,

I very much regret to write this letter to Your Excellency.

It concerns our seminarian Mr. Aloysius Schwartz which we had hoped to call to the priesthood this June 29th in his own parish, St. Martin's in Washington.

This April 1957, at the end of the 2nd term and during Easter holidays, Mr. Schwartz was ill and he showed signs of false mysticism together with psychopathology troubles.

He told his friends seminarians [sic] that he was going to die on Holy Friday, he refused to take the drugs the doctor has prescribed which would be a very little thing if it was not accompanied by Mr. Schwartz's ideas of refusing also some food to share the sufferings and starvation of the poor people on [sic] the world; this attitude was not controlled either by a spiritual advisor, Superior or Doctor. This semi-fasting had been going on for weeks already.

When we came to be aware of all this, it suddenly gave us anxiety about his psychism.

As things were already arranged, "omnia parata sunt", we let Mr. Schwartz go back to the States, praying and hoping for the best.

But yesterday, June 11, new facts came to our knowledge which convinced us finally that Mr. Schwartz had to be stopped just before his ordination. Thus the matter which had been discussed several times by the Seminary Council since April came this morning to this drastic decision.

It is clear that Mr. Schwartz had come to grave breaches of trust.

He has taken steps against the very spirit of his missionary vocation and to undermine the legitimate authority. The facts we know now give a light on many little attitudes of criticism and lack of optimism and apostolic mind we had noticed previously without being confronted with the real meaning of all of this.

We cannot undertake the responsibility of letting him be promoted further in the Orders.

The very question of his membership of our Society shall be submitted to the Most Reverend Bishop Kerkhofs of Liege, Superior Major of the Society.

We are writing directly to Mr. Schwartz (enclosed a copy in French of our letter to him).

We are very sorry for the disturbance we caused to Your Excellency and to St. Martin's Parish. May I ask your Excellency to give notice to the parish priest, Monsignor L.F. Miltenberger.

I remain,
Respectfully Yours in Our Lord,
Dieudonné Bourguignon
Superior General of the SAM[8]

Bishop O'Boyle and Al may have opened their letters from Bou on the same June day. Below is Al's letter from Father Bourguignon (which declines to mention his supposedly excessive Lenten practices):

My dear Al,

This is a very difficult letter to write. We have prayed, reflected, consulted all those who, because of their duty, could judge the question with the hope of being enlightened by God. The Council of the SAM then took the decision not to proceed with your ordination as a priest.

We are fully aware of the gravity of this decision, at a time when all the arrangements have been made. We believe in our conscience that we would assume a heavy responsibility before the Holy Church in acting otherwise.

I wish to specify the decisive element is not the letter which you write to me on 29 May, and which I have first of all simply filed. However, the content of that letter has become clearer in the context of your actions and attitudes, as perceived by us in concrete terms.

At the time of your oath, you declared, "wishing to collaborate with my brother missionaries to achieve the special objectives set for us by the Church ... I swear to devote myself to the objective of the Société des Auxiliaires des Missions .... I pledge to the Superiors of the Society obedience and submission according to the Constitutions."

Instead of that, you have adopted an attitude calculated to denigrate the superiors; you endeavor to divert your brothers from their vocation; you act and speak not as a member of our group, but as an enemy, plotting against the Society, mounting conspiracies. At a time

[8] *Pos*, 322–23.

when you appeal to the confidence of the superiors, you betray their confidence, you are disloyal and encourage others to be disloyal in the most absolute way.

In addition to this, you pretend illegitimately to speak in the name of God. No duty, no sacramental grace allows you to dictate to others how they should behave. In this area, you are totally deluded.

The spirit displayed by you would make your presence with a native bishop dangerous. It runs strongly counter to that of Fr. Lebbe.

We had hoped that the concerns that your behavior at the seminary had often caused in the past were not deep-seated. But your attitude over the last two months has revealed to us the seriousness of your errors. We pray to God that you may understand the gravity not only of your acts, but above all, of your inner and spiritual attitude.

We must warn you that your case will be referenced to the Major Superior of the Society in accordance with the articles 219, 220, and 222 of our Constitutions.

Please believe me that we share your sorrow and that we are concerned about your state of mind after this. We will consider carefully your reply.

May God be with you.
D. Bourguignon
Superior General SAM[9]

We do not know the state of Al's mind when he read Bou's letter kicking him out of the Samists. However, two of his siblings, Lou and his youngest sister, Joan, spent a great deal of time with Al in the days that followed his reception of the news, and they said their brother didn't seem the slightest bit bothered. In Al's innumerable homilies, reflections, retreats, and conversations over the three decades that followed—venues where he often revealed past crises, tragedies, and other intimate stories—he never spoke about this period of extreme trial.

As his ordination twisted wildly in the wind, Al's siblings saw a man not caught in a tide of despair, but composed and prayerful. To Lou and Joan, Al seemed to understand that the situation with Bou would be handled by something outside of himself. One thing Al was firm on, though, was that he had his part to play to make

[9] Pos, 323–24.

firm the calling God had set into him as a child. He would have to cooperate to help salvage his shipwrecked vocation. He would need to return to Belgium.

LACKING THE AIRFARE, Al's father begged a friend on his son's behalf. Within a week, Al was on a plane back to Belgium to piece together the crumbling walls of his mission. His first stop was to his old spiritual director, Canon Gustave Thils, who said he would do whatever was necessary to buoy up what he was confident would become a holy priesthood. Thils encouraged Al to arrange a face-to-face meeting with His Excellency Louis-Joseph Kerkhofs, the bishop of Liège, who was the superior major of SAM. Thils urged Al to speak plainly to the bishop, an approach that had never been problematic for Al.

A few days later, Al pleaded his case to Kerkhofs, hoping for the bishop's beneficence in considering his momentary lapse in judgment in sending the letter. It is thought that he laid out his differences of opinion with Bou and explained that his representative duty as "Senior Student to the Superior" had placed him in a vulnerable position. He shared that he had just graduated magna cum laude and was the first American ever to complete formation with the Samists. He gave his reasons for leaving the Maryknolls, his aspiration to a more forsaken path to serve God in feeding and watering the uncatechized souls of the poor. He had a particular desire, he told him, to serve within the war-torn mission fields of South Korea.

Then, it is thought, he spoke of the woman he loved. He shared with Bishop Kerkhofs his devotion and deep-rooted love for Our Lady of Banneux, Belgium's Virgin of the Poor, as she had called herself. In fact, it had been Kerkhofs who investigated and authenticated this Marian apparition, and actively promoted devotion to her. The bishop took it upon himself to set up the commission of theologians, doctors, and psychiatrists to interview Mariette Beco, the eleven-year-old peasant girl from the village of Banneux who claimed she saw the Mother of God on eight occasions, beginning at nightfall on January 15, 1933. Also interviewed were individuals who claimed that the spring waters unearthed by Mary in Banneux healed maladies including skull fractures, deafness, a broken jaw, cerebrospinal meningitis, and paralysis. Twenty miracles were confirmed between 1933 and 1938. Thanks largely to Kerkhofs' work, on August 22, 1949, Pope Pius XII formally approved the authenticity of the apparitions. Perhaps it was when Al expressed his closeness to Our Lady of Banneux that the winds began to turn in his favor. Both men experienced what seemed a gravitational pull to Our Lady at her apparition site; both understood that truly serving Mary meant obliging the grinding and unsentimental work of rescuing the poor from their isolation and misery.

While the Liège bishop was considering Al's fate, at least one SAM priest raced to Al's rescue. His old buddy Father Guch showed demonstrable support for his American colleague, who had often overwhelmed him with good cheer, intellect, and his desire to become holy. The following is an excerpt from a letter that de Guchteneer (Father Stephen Murakabe would later become his adopted Japanese name) wrote to Father Bourguignon:

> [Al] was, not only for me, but for several others I could name, an example of spiritual life, prayer and courage and the true spirit of SAM. His spirit of poverty, his renunciation, his simplicity, his spirit of adaptation were the edification of the whole seminary.... If your decision [to stop his ordination] is based on a so-called spirit of rebellion, a lack of obedience, pretension, pride ... on the part of Al, perhaps it is you who is mistaken.
>
> The fact that you have taken this decision at the last minute is also astonishing. If Al's failings are really so serious that they are an obstacle to his ordination, it is extremely strange that you only realized this 15 days before his ordination!!! But perhaps it is the letter that Al wrote to you on the boat which suddenly [made your decision for you]. Which opened your eyes? I have not read that letter, but Al spoke about it at length with me when he arrived in New York. I am one hundred percent in agreement with what Al had the courage to say to you.... (But do you know the reasons? And if you know them, are you capable of understanding them?) I am sure that many other SAM members are of the same opinion, but perhaps they do not have the courage to be honest with themselves, and above all the courage to say openly to the competent authority what they are thinking, which is the very basis of the *system of confidence* [italics his], unless I am mistaken.[10]

[10] *Pos*, 327–28.

Two days later, on June 18, 1957, Father de Guchteneer composed another stinging rebuke regarding Bou's questioning of Al's mental state. He had spoken with Archbishop O'Boyle of Washington, who found it strange that the superior general had not intervened to help the "mad" Al Schwartz far sooner than "15 days before his scheduled orientation". De Guchteneer went on ironically:

> I suppose that before making such a judgment about Al ... you asked him to undergo an in-depth psychiatric examination. I suppose that you questioned at length the seminarians, who know each other better than any superior can ever know them. (But do you have confidence in the judgement of a seminarian?) ... I suppose that you also questioned his director of conscience, Canon G. Thils, and that the latter provided you with a long report on the subject. You have, I am sure, contacted the director of the American College, not to speak of the other seminarians, who have known and been able to appreciate Al.

Lamenting the "strain" of the seminary environment under Bou's leadership, he finally paid high tribute to Schwartz, claiming, "I would like to have just some of the holiness of Al."[11]

After some consideration, an unconventional but Solomonic compromise was hatched by Bishop Kerkhofs. He asked Bou to dismiss Al from the oath he'd taken to serve under the banner of the Société des Auxiliaires des Missions. Kerkhofs, in fact, now wanted him in his own diocese. He was free to become a priest, incardinated in Liège. The bishop signed the appropriate paperwork on June 22, 1957, and told Al to get back home to Washington. He had his ordination to attend.

But on the way, Al had one last stop to make. It would be the most significant stop of his life.

---

[11] *Pos*, 329–30.

5

Virgin of the Poor

Banneux and Priestly Ordination, June 1957

HE TRAVELED SOUTHEAST BY TRAIN, as he had so many times before, passing by slender brooks that zig-zagged into the farming communities from Wallonia's steep-sided hills. The cashmere blanket of the Ardennes mountain range began to stretch out and rise before him; the rolling green fortress seemed to Al to wrap its protective arms around that speck of a town called Banneux. The landscape had been carved indelibly into his mind.

When he stepped away from the small country train station to begin walking to his reprieve of Banneux, he always thought of the disregarded village of Nazareth. To Al, when Mary appeared to Mariette Beco in this backwater village in 1933, she had chosen to touch down at a place similar to where she raised the child Jesus. *Can anything good come out of Nazareth?* Not even Belgian cartographers thought to include the name of Banneux on their maps. It was a town World War I German soldiers didn't notice on their westward march.

But the town drew Al to it, as a sunflower bends to the sun's rays. By the time he was in his second year at Louvain, Banneux had become a part of his soul. When his stomach ailment flared or his head colds worsened, or Bou had become too much, Al thought of the town and of Mary, who rose in him like a small flame, and his mind would churn, *How can I get there?*

Before catching his plane back to America to be ordained a priest in the summer of 1957, he returned to this place of his healing one last time.

When over the years he was asked about his attraction to the small apparition site in Belgium, Father Al always said that Mary had been calling for him from Banneux since he was a child in D.C. The Beco home, which still stands today in the shadow of where Mary appeared, was very similar to his own childhood home—humble, full of brothers and sisters, with the head of the household always struggling to make ends meet, next to other homes in largely the same situation.

MARIETTE BECO'S FATHER, Julien, was a hard-luck wiremaker who often was forced to support his eleven children off the land. The little garden in his front yard was his family's sustenance. He never made it to Mass on Sundays, which meant his family stayed home as well. Other than one small image of Our Lady, the Beco home could have been mistaken for a pagan's house. As everyday travails, financial issues, and other impediments stacked up in Julien's life, so did an erosion of his belief in the teachings of the Catholic faith. God seemed galaxies away to him. Sadly, the image of a distant God was shared by several other poor families in Banneux. Father Al would compare the spiritually impoverished town to the once-lukewarm village of Ars, which Saint John Vianney was forced to set right after much of the Catholic flock was guillotined in the French Revolution.

Banneux was not unlike other country villages throughout Europe in the 1930s, a time when indifference to the Catholic faith spread along with the push for industrialization in urban areas. Employment opportunities in the city enticed countrymen to find livelihoods away from their homes, where punishing hours in factories weakened their bodies, battered their souls, and tore at the once-harmonious fabric of family life. Banneux had a population of three hundred, many of whom had fallen away from the sacraments. It was the unspoken mental stain of the townsfolk; they knew where they were supposed to be on Sunday, but they just didn't seem to care. The situation was especially egregious in light of the town's then-recent history. In 1914, the villagers made a collective vow to consecrate Banneux to Our Lady if she would spread her mantle over their town when German soldiers began their Belgian routes during World War I. Banneux townsfolk never heard a single rifle shot.

Mariette Beco had a reputation for being a sweet and caring child who looked after her many little brothers and sisters. Like her father, she was frank in correcting her siblings and even her schoolmates. She never lied. She was athletic, rarely losing in foot races, including those against red-faced boys who were her age or older. Similar to the children to whom Our Lady appeared at her apparitions in Fatima and Lourdes, Mary seemed to choose Mariette simply because she was poor and had an open heart.

The apparitions began when Mariette noticed a glow in her own front yard. It shone on Sunday, January 15, 1933, a frigid and windy winter evening. She was kneeling on a wooden bench in the small parlor and pressing her nose against a frosty window pane in her house. One of her little brothers, ten-year-old Julien Jr., hadn't made it home. Belgian winter skies begin to darken at three P.M. in January; it was seven P.M., and all that shone on that moonless night was faint starlight. She wanted to go out in search of Julien, whose supper she had been keeping, but her mother, Louise, told her to help care for another sickly brother who was crying in his crib.

Then a "bright ball" like the moon passed through pine trees and began to move toward the Beco home, gradually taking on the silhouette of an exceedingly beautiful woman. She was a little over five feet in height and hovered a few feet above the ground just outside the window. The image looked directly at Mariette. She was smiling. No one else in the home was the wiser as to what was unfolding.

She appeared as a vision of radiant light, clothed in a white garment above a blanket of snow, where an onion patch would bloom in the springtime. She stood in a posture of motherly love, her head slightly inclined to the left. After gawking at the luminosity of the image for several minutes, Mariette thought to place the oil lamp in another room, imagining a reflected play of light was being cast. But the image of the beautiful woman remained, even getting brighter. When she bolted for the door to greet the woman, explaining what she had seen, her mother told her to stay inside because of the darkness and cold. Superstitions were widespread in the Belgian countryside towns of those days, and her mother instinctively attributed the glow to that of a witch. The light from the front yard was extinguished.

Mariette went to her room later that night and began to pray the Rosary. It would mark her return to the practice of the faith. She began to attend weekday Mass, seek catechism instruction, and practice habits of virtue and piety.

Three days later, Mary returned. Mariette had been out seeking her in temperatures well below freezing, and Mary, with a tender expression, smiled and coaxed her to the edge of a deep forest at the Becos' property line. As Mariette walked through the night, illuminated by the moon, Mariette's father, who had seen her puzzling behavior from indoors, raced outside for her. Thereafter, he watched his daughter drop like a stone three times onto the frozen ground, where she knelt for a sustained period and appeared to look up into a point in space. She seemed irradiated, completely absorbed, he thought, in a supernatural trance. About 125 yards from their home, he watched Mariette kneel by a spring he had never seen before. He was too afraid to speak when she suddenly plunged her hands into the icy water. He didn't know that she was obliging the odd command of Mary, who had told Mariette, "Plunge your hands into this water.... The spring is reserved for me." She kept her hands submerged for a long time.

When Mariette released her reddened hands from the spring, she began to follow Mary down a narrow road. Her father asked, "Where are you going?", to which Mariette responded, "She is calling me." It was then that Julien, who could not see the vision, rushed to find the parish priest at his rectory; within days he, too, would return to the full practice of the Catholic faith, which he had abandoned long ago when hard times fell on his impoverished family.

A few nights later, Mary appeared again and introduced herself to Mariette as "the Virgin of the Poor", the first time in history that Our Lady had identified herself with those living in poverty. In the days that followed, the Blessed Mother told Mariette she had come to alleviate the sufferings of the poor and broken-spirited, while repeatedly emphasizing the need for unceasing prayer.

Mary asked Mariette to request that a small chapel be built in Banneux. She knew the town had mostly departed from the faith and needed an activating point of renewal. Within a year, the entire town returned to the practice of the Catholic faith.

IT COULD BE ARGUED that the language of heaven Mary brought to Banneux was not, in practicality, destined only for the peasant

Mariette, but also for Venerable Aloysius Schwartz. During the early years of his priesthood, Father Al would spend untold hours in contemplation of her few words (less than eighty in total). Turning over the messages from Mary's eight apparitions in his head, he would piece together a system that would structure his own incomprehensibly fruitful work for the poor.

First of all, he beheld divine significance in Our Lady's unsubtle request that Mariette stick her hands in a near-freezing spring. He regarded it as a Marian invitation to enter into the humiliations of her Son, as well as an encouragement to take up penances to help convert sinners—a message made clear at Fatima in 1917. Father Al would eventually incorporate Mary's request for mortifications into his own missionary identity. Equally important, Our Lady's insistence on prayer and the lessening of burdens became the cornerstone of Father Al's Boystowns and Girlstowns. He wholly understood that when Mary identified herself as the Virgin of the Poor, she had proclaimed herself to be a champion for those scarred by their privation. He, too, would hold fast in his fidelity to the brokenhearted and poverty-stricken. The construction of the humble chapel was another element of Banneux that touched Father Al, and he would see to it that other simple chapels, modeled after that of the Virgin of the Poor, would be built in Boystown and Girlstown communities throughout the world. In the hands of Aloysius Schwartz, the message at Banneux would become the raw material to build the broadest non-government-funded service for poor children in history.

In the chapel of Banneux on that day in 1957, he gave Mary his life. He vowed to her that everything he did in the days that followed he would do as her servant. He would have the ears of the marveling Cana wedding attendants, who heeded Mary when she said, "Do whatever he tells you". Al would do whatever Jesus commanded, but the command would come through Mary. No one was on hand to witness it, but perhaps Al lay down prostrate near the spot where Our Lady first appeared to Mariette Beco twenty-four years earlier. What we do know is that he consecrated to the Virgin of the Poor his priesthood; he would be her servant. Because Al often kept private the inner workings of his heart, he never fully shared what unfolded on that day. But he attributed to Our Lady of Banneux the salvation of his priesthood. "In a sense, She was the one who ordained me", he wrote. "She puts Her hands on this child and blesses this child. Through the bishop, Our Lady did this to me."[1]

Surrendering his life to Mary's Immaculate Heart, Al left Banneux with a new motivation. To honor his Queen, he would strive to orient his priesthood to the rawest form of Christ's gospel call to serve the poor. He would later write:

> Mary of Banneux chose me at an early age just as she erupted in the night in the life of Mariette Beco. She suddenly appeared in my life without any preparation. She brought me to Belgium where I discovered her. I never heard of Banneux before then. So my priesthood in a special way belongs to Our Lady of Banneux. My apostolate is hers and I would like to be buried at her feet and say that all praise, glory, and honor for anything good accomplished in my life goes to her and her alone.[2]

As the numberless storm clouds gathered around him over the next thirty-five years, he would return interiorly to that warm memory from Banneux. A mental image of the Virgin of the Poor remained his safe port for the remainder of his life. In his very last hours, Father Al would call out to her, whispering aloud to the Sisters of Mary who surrounded him, "The Virgin of the Poor has been working with me since the beginning. She does not need me anymore."[3]

"What he offered to Mary in Banneux was his entire priesthood, and I imagine that's as pure as it gets", said Al's brother Lou. "And I imagine that's why everything he did grew. It also grew because he wanted to be a martyr; he would never share that desire with me, but I knew it because of the saints he was drawn to. So many of them were martyrs." After pledging his priesthood to Mary—and surrendering to her all of its future merits—Al left Banneux forever. It was time for him to become a priest.

ON SATURDAY, JUNE 29, 1957, the last of *I Love Lucy*'s 181 episodes had just aired. Buddy Holly was a day or two away from releasing "Peggy Sue"; Red Sox right fielder Ted Williams, who would

---

[1] *Serm*, 1:147.
[2] PM.
[3] *Pos*, 615.

go on to bat .388 that year, was suiting up in Fenway Park's low-ceilinged clubhouse for a game against the Detroit Tigers; and Aloysius Schwartz lay fully prostrate on the marble floor of Saint Martin of Tours Church in Washington, D.C., as retired auxiliary bishop John McNamara ordained him a Roman Catholic priest on the Feast of Saints Peter and Paul—the two great missionary martyrs of the newborn Church. Earlier that day in Rome, Pope Pius XII implored Brazilian Catholic priests and laity to fight the expanding plague of leprosy in South America,[4] and Father Al would soon be on his way to Korea's leper colonies and tubercular wards. Four members of the Société des Auxiliaires des Missions community made the trip to America to join their friend for his ordination, including, of course, Guch. Just two weeks later, Bishop Kerkhofs, superior major of the Samists, would write to Father Al to tell him that even his old superior Father Bou was happy with the solution they had found and had "realized that [his] behavior toward you was unfitting".[5] Every member of Al's large extended family attended his ordination, too, including many of those same aunts, uncles, and cousins who had done everything in their power to keep him from Belgium years before.

In that crowd at Saint Martin, one person stood proudest: Louis Schwartz—the once-poor kid from Baltimore who, watching his son rise from the floor as a priest of God, suddenly felt himself the richest man in Washington, D.C.

---

[4] Pius XII, Address to the Brazilian Association of Assistance to the Leprous (June 29, 1957), http://www.vatican.va/content/pius-xii/pt/speeches/1957/documents/hf_p-xii_spe_19570629_malatti-lebbra.html.

[5] Quoted in *Pos*, 566.

6

"Now, *Sinbunim*, You Know What It
Is Like to Be Poor"

Arrival and Devastation in South Korea, 1957–1958

FATHER AL ARRIVED IN SEOUL, South Korea, on December 8, 1957, the Feast of the Immaculate Conception.

He stood there like Ichabod Crane, momentarily startled and fence-post skinny inside a wind-whipped cassock, his sharp, dominant nose seemingly pointing to what was unfolding before him. An exhausted-looking boy, unnoticed by Seoul's morning passersby, zombied up a frozen path with a small girl, about three years old, tied to his back. She resembled a clump of unwashed clothes. Her hair was matted and had fallen out in patches. Father Al knew she was sick. The boy's thin cotton clothing looked to have just sopped up mud. The priest's heart was wrung.

As the boy walked closer to Father Al, he abruptly stopped in the midst of the hustle and bustle of the frigid morning. After the boy's body careened unsteadily, he caught himself, then he slowly lay down on his side, so as to not smother the small girl. It seemed to be a good place to die. The sunken-eyed boy watched the soles of shoes parade past in a whir. A few people crouched down to speak to him and even offered him some money; eventually a woman dragged the pulverized boy like a rag doll to his feet. He and the girl wandered off and disappeared before Father Al knew even what to do.

"The expression of the boy's face, [it was] an expression which contained all the unselfconscious, uncomplaining, unquestioning sorrow and grief of the world", Father Al described. "He stared indifferently ahead of him with a passive, hurt-animal look."[1]

The twenty-eight-year-old American missionary had been in Seoul for just an hour and was awaiting the train that would transport him to his new existence in Busan at the southern tip of the country. He had nothing but his faith, a duffel bag, and six hours to kill. The rawness of the morning and long-traveling winds from the plains of Manchuria in northern China chilled his uncovered body parts.

Many years later, he thought back to his first hour in Korea. "It looked like the end of the world. Everywhere I looked I could see squalor, shacks, shanties, slums, and refugees", he wrote. "I remember passing a beggar on a street corner, wrapped in rags, his hand outstretched, rocking softly back and forth, and whispering to himself, 'a chuwo, a chuwo' (so cold, so cold)."[2]

He decided to warm his bones with a long walk into the countryside. After some time, he seemed to have opened a gate and stepped past an invisible border wall into a dark moonscape. Before him was a broken-hearted kingdom of war refugees, living in what seemed an endless landscape of hopelessness. It was a village crisscrossed with networks of narrow paths that led to one-room hovels pieced together with scraps of wood, tar paper, canvas, cardboard, and tin—whatever would act as impromptu adhesives. Faces everywhere peered out at him from squatters' huts, shriveled tents, and lean-tos thrown together on top of black sludge. He saw a large city rat drag its swollen body out of putrefied water, look about, and disappear back into the slime. The toxic scent of sewage, decaying animals, and human waste scorched his nostrils. As he walked on mercifully inventorying the vast population of the poor, a thought surged in his heart—these multitudes were the mortified body of Jesus Christ. He stood in awe; he now knew the byproduct of war.

"It is easier to believe Jesus Christ present in an immaculate, richly ornate tabernacle", Father Al would reflect in his book *Poverty*, "or to believe him present in words written on clean germ-free pages, or again to believe him present in the impressive, solemn Magisterium of the Church, than to believe him present in the unwashed

---

[1] *StSi*, 26.
[2] PM.

masses of poverty-stricken humanity." He continued: "It requires faith of the deepest kind, a faith similar to that of the Centurion on Calvary. The Centurion looked up at the crushed figure of Christ upon the cross, a figure in whom there was neither beauty nor comeliness, and said: 'Indeed, this was the son of God.'"[3]

On a pensive walk back toward the city, Father Al stopped at a tumbledown food stand in an alley. He pushed out his first smile in Korea when he saw a Baby Ruth candy bar. *America.* He reached into his pocket and gave the clerk some hwan. He unwrapped the bar, took a bite, and instantly spit it out of his mouth. He tossed the remainder of the stale and moldy candy into a pile of trash. A girl instantly ran up, picked it out, and devoured it. His face reddened. America was yesterday; it wasn't *his* any longer.

As he waited for his train to arrive, a canopy of silver stars began to spread across the clear, cold sky. He studied the sky and considered it a mercy for the Korean poor that wallowed in filth beneath it. With night came a warming memory of his Korean friend and Louvain classmate, Father John Chang, who had promised to greet him upon his arrival in Busan early the next morning. He recalled a time when Father Chang shed tears over the unique and mysterious elegance of Korea's night sky. "The sky in my country never grows black", Chang told Father Al when they were seminarians. "It deepens from one shade of blue to another until it reaches a perfect shade and depth of dark blue, then the stars come out and begin to shine. Really, I have seen nothing as beautiful as the night sky of Korea."[4]

The culture-shocked priest finally boarded a shunting steam train that would dive into Korea's deep south, seemingly another world away from the capital of Seoul. After settling into his second-class section of the slow-moving train, he observed the smattering of passengers in his quiet car. Most met his eyes with a melancholy stare. Some gazed with vacant eyes at a fixed point in space that he found himself to be at the end of. He turned to look outside his window and saw a countryside and treeless mountainscape bathed in moonlight, spread out as silent and untroubled as Bethlehem at midnight.

[3] *Pov*, 84.
[4] *StSi*, 28.

After finally dozing off, he was jolted awake at 3:30 in the morning by a paroxysm as ten or so boys raced into his train car while it was stopped at a station. "It was though someone had emptied a pack of caged rodents in the car", he wrote of his first night in Korea.

> In an instant, the boys were racing down the aisles, scurrying under seats, and reaching between the legs of passengers for discarded pop bottles, scraps of food, and cigarette butts. They pushed food hungrily down their mouths then washed it down with what remained in the pop bottles.... The boys were uniformly filthy and in rags, and their eyes burned with a fierce, scared, hunted-animal expression.... One of the boys' faces had been beaten black and blue; another had a running ulcer just under the nose; another boy's face was grotesquely wrinkled and disfigured like that of an old, old man. When the conductor appeared in the doorway, the boys scampered out of the car in near-panic, carrying their spoils with them. The whole episode had happened so quickly that it had an unreal and apocalyptic, almost nightmarish quality about it.[5]

It was a diabolic image that never left him. He couldn't have known then that the demented scene was a foreshadowing of his priesthood. The southbound train was carrying him to bridge underpasses, rat-infested alleyways, countryside gullies, and bleak state-run homes, where endless lines of orphans and forsaken souls awaited him. His priesthood would center on pulling boys and girls from abuse, horror, and utter desolation.

He arrived bleary-eyed at the station before daybreak, where Father Chang, the vicar general of the diocese, raced up to him at the railway platform with a delegation of about a hundred applauding Catholics in tow. A young girl approached Busan's newest priest and handed him an enormous bouquet of flowers. He was overwhelmed. People just gawked at him at this "homecoming". Within minutes, he was hurried away in a speeding jeep that came to a stop in a church parking lot. Father Chang led him directly into the sacristy of a Church where he asked Father Al to vest for Mass.

"I could feel a hundred pairs of eyes burning the side of my face, taking in the difference of complexion, color of hair, and length of

---

[5] *StSi*, 29–30.

nose", he said. "I was a stranger in a strange land, and for the first time since my arrival in Korea, I felt it."[6] Yet at the same time, "it was a Mass of thanksgiving. I felt 13 years of preparation, that I had finally arrived."[7]

In 1957, the Diocese of Busan sorely lacked Catholic priests; Father Al was its lone American priest, and he didn't speak the language. Before the civil war that started in 1950, just twenty thousand of the four hundred thousand plus souls in Busan identified as Catholics. Since the end of the war in 1953, shell-shocked Koreans had begun surging to God, and many to the Catholic faith. Catechumens seemed to be around every corner; more than five thousand were preparing to enter the Church when Father Al arrived. The number of Catholics had quadrupled in the four years since the war, including ten thousand who had entered the Church in 1956. Bishop John Choi had only fifty priests to feed his entire flock; he needed Father Al to get to work. The growing Catholic population was starving for a priest to administer to them the sacraments, and tens of thousands of war refugees and social rejects were just plain starving. Father Al clearly understood what was expected of him. His future included long days of service to the Korean people and the Church; he began the habit of further intensifying his prayer, extending it deep into the night, to make certain that his work the following morning, in whatever form it took, would not be hollowed out.

"The honeymoon, the romance, the glamour of being in a foreign land with its different sights, sounds, and smells lasts but a few weeks", he said. "Then begins the day-to-day grind of mastering a new language, and the day-in, day-out struggle of accustoming oneself to a new way of living. To become one of them and one with them is the task of a lifetime and, I have been told, it is not child's play."[8]

Within a few days, Father Al met a young Korean man named Damiano Park, who had been studying English literature in college. Park agreed to become his interpreter and tutor as the newly arrived priest accepted the task of attempting to master one of the most difficult languages in the world. Park became one of Father Al's best

---

[6] *StSi*, 31.
[7] PM.
[8] *StSi*, 32.

friends, one who often could be seen by his side for the remainder of his life.

A few days after meeting one another, the pair left the rectory at daybreak and walked the long bridge that stretched from Busan onto Yeongdo, an island notorious for its several thousands of terraced shacks built onto a mountainside. The huts were almost indistinguishable from the mud-brown mountain on which they were located. To Father Al, this bridge acted as a metaphor; it struck him that setting foot onto the island of Yeongdo represented the first day of the remainder of his life. This was his turning to Jerusalem; it was where he could finally enter to bear the cross of the societally leprous and offer his priesthood as a crucifixion to unite himself with them. He stopped on a span of the bridge, lingered a bit, and began to pray.

"Father was wearing an old navy overcoat over his cassock. He probably wore that coat for about 10 more years until the Sisters of Mary bought him a new one", Park remembered. "We were in the middle of the bridge.... You could see not only the downtown but also the slopes of bare mountains where there were thousands of shacks and squatter huts." He continued: "Fr. Al was leaning against the guard rail of the bridge and attentively looking at the shabbily clothed people walking over the bridge with their stooped bodies against the cold winter sea and [wind] blowing against their rough faces. He looked very serious.... He seemed to become resolved that he would proclaim the Good News of salvation to them."[9]

As they ascended the winding path to the tiny homes of cliff dwellers, the pair was forced to step over thin streams of grayish water that flowed toward the bay like thin, steaming oatmeal. They eventually walked into a community of hundreds of mountainside hovels perched on inconceivably sloping angles, many of which were held up by bamboo stilts "that defied the laws of physics", Father Al later said.[10] As the priest and his friend entered the homes of the cliff dwellers, one by one, he discovered a solemn and anxious population strangled by appalling conditions—tuberculosis, scarcity of food, despair, faithlessness, and various illnesses brought on by Korea's merciless winter winds. All over the mountainside was the echo of

---

[9] Damiano Park, *Father Al Schwartz, Who Is Still Alive* (self-pub.), 15–16.
[10] *Starved*, p. 34.

people coughing. The first tent into which he crawled was filled with four men afflicted with tuberculosis. The gusts of clean air from the Sea of Japan instantly became overwhelmed by the smell of disease, putrefied garbage, sweat, and human waste.

The American priest inhaled. It was the smell of home.

Sixteen years after movements in his boyhood heart began to point him toward the friendless life of a missionary, Father Al could finally articulate in action what had perhaps begun to ripple within him as a child at yellow-bricked Holy Name Elementary in D.C., 7,100 miles away: *Oh Jesus, allow me now to enter well into the sweet violence of poverty.* In his soul, the path up the mountain seemed like a red carpet crowning his marriage to innumerable days of dry martyrdom; his home was now in the midst of lonesome, unmarked places—in garbage-dump homes, cruel government-run tubercular wards, and shanties outside his rectory where the insane lived. Here Father Al could effectively crawl into the skin of Jesus Christ the Starved Man.

In seminary, Al had been jolted by British poet Edith Sitwell's depiction of Christ as a "Starved Man" in her poem "Still Falls the Rain". Nailed to the Cross, Christ observes a German air squadrons' merciless bombardment of London in 1940. An excerpt:

Still falls the Rain
At the feet of the Starved Man hung upon the Cross
Christ that each day, each night, nails there, have mercy on us—
. . .
Still falls the Blood from the Starved Man's wounded Side:
He bears in His Heart all wounds,—those of the light that died,
The last faint spark
In the self-murdered heart, the wounds of the uncomprehending
    dark[11]

Sitwell takes inventory of humanity's gruesome tendencies—its pride, greed, black-heartedness, and shameful behaviors—embodied in the machinations of war. Bombs are made analogous to our sins against Christ, dropped as "blind as the nineteen hundred and forty nails upon the Cross". It is only through Jesus' spilled Blood, Sitwell

---

[11] Edith Sitwell, *Collected Poems* (London: Macmillan, 1965), 272–73.

contends, that grace and love are made incarnate. The redemption of
humanity, Al saw in the poem, would be found both through God's
mercy and through those willing to *starve*—even die—as an expiation
for a sinful world.

Looking at the desolate Korean mountainside, Father Al understood that he—with Stillwell's Starved Man looking out on bomb-
cratered London—was part of the Body of Christ meant to gaze
upon God's crushed ones. These people lived in the "uncomprehending dark", caught within an unchangeable soap opera of disor-
der, their souls parched, broken, and craving Christ's spilled Blood.
Reading the poem in seminary, Father Al had wondered whether he
too would need to be torn to pieces, scattered about, stretched out
into the far-flung places of mendicants—to die like Christ in order
to heal. Or was he called simply to be a faithful and hard-working
parish missionary priest? Here in Korea, he sensed it was the former.
He understood immediately that if he failed to meet the poor as a
"starved man", he would expose himself as an imposter. "Christ himself was marked by the sign of poverty. He was born under it, lived
under it, died under it", he wrote later. "The historical Christ chose
to be poor and a concomitant fact is, his disciples have no choice
but to follow."[12]

With Damiano by his side on the mountain that day, Father
Al began pulling back the flaps of tents and occasionally crawling
onto the ground to enter the low doorways of shacks. He introduced himself as *So Jae Geon* (which translates to "is rebuilding").
As Lebbe had changed his name to become one with the Chinese, so did Father Al with the South Koreans. He laughed as some
referred to him instead as *khojaengi*, which means "big nose". He
entered one cave-like structure filled with eleven boys who lived
as ragpickers. Most of them were asleep on a dirt floor. Their living space was twelve feet long and six feet wide; to sleep they had
to curl into odd positions to conform to the space. A day's work,
Father Al learned, earned them four cents, which bought enough
rice to survive that day.

"Sitting there on the dirt floor, I looked up through the dim light
at the circle of faces about me. The faces all indicated that they had

[12] *Pov*, 17.

not come into contact with soap and water for some time", Father Al reflected. "They were forced to lead a hand-to-mouth, dog-eat-dog existence and it showed. It was visible in the expression on their faces and the look in their eyes."[13]

Throughout the day, Damiano watched the American priest warm decrepit homes by reminding the poor of their forgotten identity: they were loved by God. Looking back years later, the Korean translator claimed that "the Holy Spirit had descended upon him". Father Al seemed to Damiano to be a saint. Wherever he set foot on the mountain, people gawked at him—partly because he was a white man, but also because his eyes looked into their own with sincere love. They could tell he would be coming back for them.

When the sun began to set, the pair turned back to the city. Damiano cleared his throat and spoke a single sentence to the tired priest: "Now, *Sinbunim*"—meaning "Father"—"you know what it is like to be poor in Korea."[14]

In the days that followed, Father Al considered more deeply the reality of the lives of the poor he passed in the streets each day. He believed that God could shower them with miracles, sustenance, and endless measures of his grace. But he also knew that until they experienced God through the witness of those willing to enter fully into the cave of their poverty—willing to *become* them—their poorness would maintain its hold. These hundreds of thousands of war-ravaged Koreans, and the dark communities where they resided, required one-on-one, flesh-and-blood witnesses of God's love; they needed to be rescued. They, too, were capable of God's inheritance. Father Al also knew, of course, that the slums would forever remain as unvisited colonies of lepers unless someone resembling Christ stepped into them. Milquetoast compromises fashioned from godless welfare assistance or social justice help would fall far short of the mandate that had been resounding within him for many years. There had to be a cost to save, a crucifixion.

He would later observe: "Christ really did little to relieve directly and massively the material misery of the people among whom he lived.... When Christ healed and helped in the Gospels, it was

[13] *StSi*, 37.
[14] *StSi*, 38.

usually at close range and with his own two hands."[15] The poor have a *capability* more transcendent than wealth and well-being:

> "Capax Dei" ("capable of God") is a description of man in his most sublime dimension. Poor little finite creature though he be, man is still able to be filled with God as a glass with wine or a room with sunlight. Man has within himself the capacity to become a child of God and to share fully in the divine life.... Granted that people who are hungry are not as receptive as people who are well-fed; nevertheless, they are capable both of hearing the Word of God and also of accepting in their heart. One would be doing the poor an injustice by stating dogmatically that they are incapable of learning about God, praying, or grasping, in some manner at least, the eternal truths of salvation.[16]

Much later, when Father Al found time to step away from his slum parish in the neighborhood of Song-do, he and Damiano would disappear into disregarded places throughout Korea's southeastern peninsula. He tended to ill-nourished bodies crumpled on sidewalks, insane men in cardboard boxes, and dying men shivering beneath the Busan Bridge. "Father Al was visiting people who lived like animals", said Monsignor Golasinski, who after reading Father Al's 1970 book *Poverty* was moved to serve alongside him in Korea for ten years. "Korea had been ripped in two, and he was there to see it. He saw things no one sees."

One day Father Al asked Damiano to take him to Korea's interior, where he knew poverty was even greater. They traveled eighty miles north to the village of Nam-sa, where Damiano's family lived. No villager there had ever seen a priest. Father Al was invited to stay in a small thatched cottage with no furniture. He, like everyone else in the village, slept on a quilt on an earthen floor and dined at a low table on seaweed soup, barley, and boiled eggs. Everyone seemed to have just one change of clothing. He watched boys in the hills reach their hands into cold streams in search of snails for food, a great delicacy the villagers offered to the visiting Catholic priest.

In their stark poverty, far from the din of Busan's noise and smokestacks, the villagers witnessed to a steady and harmonious rhythm of

[15] *Pov*, 131–32
[16] *Pov*, 129, 133.

order. They lived in staggeringly poor conditions, but had found great joy in their small community. Most did not even know Christ, but mysteriously to Father Al, the Holy Spirit seemed to dwell like warm light within the villagers; they were ordered by a natural law they neither knew nor could articulate. The village of Nam-sa seemed to him as ordered as the small and holy home in the scorned town of Nazareth. Everything was resplendent in its rightness: "The night, the beautiful Korean night, brings to the village a silence and peace which are almost infinite", he later described. "A breathless stillness settles over everything and the only sounds to be heard are the murmur of conversation and the soft ripple of the swiftly flowing river. There is no electricity in the village and the only light to be seen, other than that given off by moon and stars, is produced by small, dimly burning, peanut-oil lanterns."[17]

The night before his departure, Father Al was invited to a farewell celebration of singing, dancing, and storytelling. Gap-toothed villagers offered Father Al their pipes, wiping the saliva from their silver-tipped stems on filthy cotton pants that had perhaps never been washed. "He responded to their offers gladly", Damiano said. "He knew how to act as a missionary." The village storyteller began his art as the overcrowded room fell silent. A bottle of rice wine was passed around as the old man told an O. Henry–like tale that included a woodsman, a tiger, and a double-crossed Buddhist monk. The country folks fell into uproarious laughter at the surprise ending, and it seemed to Al that it would have been okay if time had stopped right then and there.

At their departure the next morning, a villager approached Father Al and Damiano with her sixteen-year-old son. In grief, she asked if they would take him into the city with them. The boy was restless and wanted to make something of himself in Busan. She had already lost two boys to the city; there had been no contact since.

"Son, do not forget your mother as your brothers have", Father Al remembered the mother saying.[18] A mother's lament were the final words he heard in Nam-sa. It was now time for him to work. His warm memory of the mountainous town would be one of his greatest consolations for many years. When Father Al returned to Busan, he

[17] *StSi*, 47.
[18] *StSi*, 49.

reflexively began spending more time caring for the orphans who lined the city's overcrowded streets. They had lost their parents in the war and were often dismissed by passersby, who seemed to regard them as wild-eyed scavengers. It is thought that the small girl on the back of the crumpled boy that first day in Seoul had plowed gullies into his memory. He would aim to become like that boy, reaching for abandoned children and carrying them on his back.

He became friends with a bright young man named Michael Rhi, who had lost his father in the war. Although Michael always presented himself as dapper in clothing and cheerful in nature, Father Al discovered that he lived in the midst of a garbage dump with his mother and small family. There within the oceanic trash heap, a widespread plague grotesquely referred to as "garbage-dump neurosis" birthed madness in men and women. Michael's older brother, Il-sun, who held an excellent job with great promise prior to the war, became afflicted by the neurosis and spoke to no one in their hut. He rarely ate the scraps of food his mother placed before him.

After spending several months attempting to help Michael gain work, an income, and physical and mental health, Father Al came to understand that the poor man had been orphaned by humanity. Michael became to Father Al a metaphor for Korea. He had just graduated third in his high school class of five hundred students, was a gifted musician, and spoke English fluently. But he had no money to attend college; he didn't even have money for food. He told Father Al: "The Church tells me to pray. Pray, that's fine. Tell me this: how can I pray when my belly is empty? Tomorrow maybe I will be dead. Then I go to heaven and when I am in heaven, then I pray. Sometimes, Father, I think maybe I lose my mind."

Michael continued. "In America people ask themselves the question: how can I make my body thin? In Korea people ask the question: how can I make my body fat? In America people wake in the morning and they ask: how can I make my life more enjoyable today? In Korea people wake in the morning and ask: how can I stay alive today?"[19]

When Michael discovered he had fallen ill with tuberculosis, doctors told him that full recovery would take two years. In tears, he

---

[19] StSi, 69, 73.

screamed at Father Al, "Please answer me this: Is God charity, or is God cruelty? … If God is charity, how can he do this to me?" His words left Father Al empty; he had no response. He offered to pay for Michael's medications, hospital bills, food, and anything that would help restore his health. He then paid for Michael's transportation to the countryside by the sea, where doctors encouraged him to remain for at least six months. On the day of his departure, Father Al pleaded with Michael to remain patient and restful, and to be as cheerful as he was able—but the priest saw a hollowed-eyed man looking back at him. "I was wasting my time", Father Al said. "He was of the sick, I was of the healthy; and a vast chasm lay between our respective worlds."[20]

A short time later, he received a letter from Michael that was shattering. With little food to eat, Michael was forced to kill and eat his lone companion, a small dog. His relatives, whom he rarely saw, worked long days in the fields and were often too tired to pay him mind. A few months after sending the letter, Michael showed up at Father Al's doorstep appearing demented. Within a few weeks, Michael was dead. Father Al believed he had lost his will to live. "[Michael] tried again and again, at times violently, to break away, to live, breathe, and be happy as everything in him cried out to do", Father Al later wrote of him. "But it was too much for him: finally, broken and exhausted, he gave up and died."[21]

Michael was the face of *the starved and the silent* of Korea. Individuals such as Michael were strewn throughout every corner of the country. They had no food. And they had no voice. Yet Father Al knew the poor like Michael were of immense eternal consequence. "The needy of the earth will rise up to judge us", Father Al once prophesied, echoing Saint John of the Cross. "*They* will decide and determine who receives eternal salvation and who receives eternal damnation."[22]

The war had killed more than one million South Koreans. To Father Al, it seemed to birth just as many street orphans. Something had to be done. He saw lonely, parentless children wherever he went.

[20] *StSi*, 84.
[21] *StSi*, 89.
[22] *TL*, 27–28.

But he also saw an open door. He knew the distressed population was drifting from Buddhism to seek other paths. He knew they could be drawn to the loving arms of Christ through the Catholic faith.

"Christ has the field to Himself here, so to speak. There is simply no competition", he wrote in his journals. "The multitude of the poor are already 'naturally Christian'; they accept a lifetime of sorrow without revolt of bitterness; they receive the mystery of pain and death with dignity and nobility ... ; they await the coming of Christ's grace as the parched rice fields await the first rain of summer. These people have first right in the Gospel. They are the privileged ones, the have-nots, the poor. At present they cry for bread and there is no one to break it for them."[23]

With this in mind, Father Al stepped into his work seeking to bring other starving Michaels to the everlasting Bread of Life. An entire population suffering the ravages of war was ignorant of Christ, and Father Al wanted to shepherd them—all he was able—to heaven.

Then his Gethsemane came.

[23] PM.

7

The Spilled Chalice

Illness and the Dawn of Korean Relief, 1958–1962

IT WAS A BITTERLY COLD MORNING as Father Al celebrated Mass in Busan's unheated cathedral. Something arose in him like a slow-moving wave, like the release of a poisonous gas within his body. He had just been handed the cruet of wine he would change into Christ's Precious Blood. After the Offertory, he felt a cold sweat cover his body and blood drain from his whitened face. He calmly placed the chalice on the corporal, steadied himself by placing his palms on the altar, and inhaled deeply. The last thing he recalled before his body collapsed beside the altar was perspiration rushing to his pores. Then all went black.

An altar boy and sacristan stood above him, spilled wine marking the floor and portions of his vestments. The chalice he had knocked to the floor had just rolled to a stop. Mass-goers may have thought their new American missionary priest had been shot. After a minute, he came to and wondered where he was.

Before he was escorted away from the altar, someone on each elbow to steady him, he saw the spilled wine and the chalice resting on its side. The image stunned him. Discombobulated, he whispered to be taken to the chalice, where he reached down and picked it up. He asked to be led back to the altar. There, he delicately folded up the corporal, neatly veiled the chalice, and closed his eyes. After shakily unvesting in the sacristy, he returned to his small room and dropped onto his narrow metal-framed, military-style bed, chilled to the bone and shivering.

"After a knock at the door, a dozen members of the parish burst into my room", he recounted in his journals. "They clunked about the room like so many mother hens, adjusting blankets, propping up pillows, pouring drinks of water, rattling off advice, and trying in general to give aid and support. I was being smothered in kindness."[1]

Father Al was suffering from a virulent case of hepatitis A, further complicated by a widespread intestinal disease. A throbbing ache took over in his liver region, where it settled like an immovable iceberg throughout the winter months. Korean doctors hypothesized that Louvain's grueling regimen, substandard and contaminated food, and sustained exposure to cold weather had worn down his body. But these first months in Korea had also been difficult. He was always cold, and since his arrival had suffered from dysentery. The day before his physical breakdown, Father Al had spent several hours in prayer in the frigid cathedral, where for a few hours he heard confessions and celebrated Mass. He slept fitfully that night but convinced himself he was well enough to celebrate Mass that morning.

A doctor encouraged complete bed rest for the next two months; he advised Father Al to refrain from even reading his Bible or speaking to anyone, unless he considered the conversation unavoidable. So the young priest spent the next sixty days in contemplative prayer and bewilderment about what had transpired, and he wondered what his future might resemble in Korea. He rarely saw anyone outside of his caretakers during this quiet period, when cold air often slipped past the edges of his thin windowpane. Although he was hopeful that sticking to his doctor's strict orders would enable his return to ministry by springtime, he continued to feel exhausted and entirely out of sorts. His malfunctioning digestive system would continue its withering course throughout the entirety of 1958.

His plight carried an uncanny similarity to that of the young curé of Ambricourt, the fictional priest from Georges Bernanos' *Diary of a Country Priest*, the 1936 classic that Father Al had read in seminary. Like the holy and misunderstood French priest portrayed in the novel, Father Al's hunger to serve his flock was blockaded by crippling stomach pains, loneliness, and feelings of despair. And like the poor curé, Father Al found himself swallowed up by inefficiency and surrounded by a cloud of gossip. When summer arrived, he sensed in the chancery a growing skepticism about his illness and an impatience with his mysteriously slow recovery. Five parishes

[1] PM.

in the Busan diocese were without priests, and Father Al was feeling the full weight of his own and others' unmet expectations. "I was a liability at the Bishop's house and the vibrations given out by the bishop and the other Korean priests who lived there became more and more hostile", he wrote in his journals. "On the surface, they were friendly enough, but it was obvious that they would be happier if I were gone."

In June, he received a letter from his aunt, Sister Melfrieda, with a premonition that his priesthood would be marked by suffering:

> My thoughts have been making many mental flights your way and each visit was accompanied by fervent prayers to our Heavenly Father to continue blessing you as He has so patently done in the past.
>
> Even if those blessings, Father Al, take the form of suffering, we can still gratefully say from the depths of our hearts, "Deo Gratias." For in permitting a share in His Passion, he is admitting us into the circle of his closest friends—His own dearly-loved Mother and his greatest Saints.
>
> So, Father Al, let us praise God and accept unreservedly any trial or cross his omniscient Wisdom deigns to send us. We will thus bring God's blessing to all our Dear Ones.[2]

By late summer, a Maryknoll religious sister and doctor encouraged the young priest to return to the United States to recuperate for as long as two years. Father Al was flabbergasted. "All I could say in protest was, 'Sister, if you only realized what a struggle it was to get here, you wouldn't say that.'"

As a compromise, he agreed to travel to Kyoto, Japan, where doctors would be better able to treat his intestinal inflammation brought on by colitis. But after a few months there, his health atrophied. He had no appetite or strength and had trouble stringing together thoughts. He wrote home saying he was "dragging along on one cylinder ... which keeps me all but incapacitated".[3]

IN DESOLATION AND TEARS, he lay in his hospital bed on a quiet night in Japan, New Year's Eve, December 1958, and penned what read

---

[2] PM.

[3] Dolores Vita, *My Brother's Witness: Msgr. Aloysius Schwartz* (West Conshohocken, PA: Infinity, 2012), 16.

like a psalm of lamentation to Mary. In this staggeringly intimate prayer, he recommitted himself and the fumes of his priesthood to his spiritual muse, the Virgin of the Poor, and fully embraced the cross of poverty he had requested from her in Banneux. The raw honesty of his plea to Mary—in a mishmash of English, French, and Latin—seems pieced together from the pure soul of a frightened child:

A la Vierge des Pauvres [To the Virgin of the Poor]:

For a long time now I have entrusted to you all that I have & all that I am. You have taken all, I have nothing. *Je suis pauvre* [I am poor].
    My health you have taken.
    My good name you have taken. I am now counted among the disobedient or psychotics or fools. I do not think I exaggerate.
    My country (Korea) you have torn from me.
    My mission vocation seems to be lost.
    My friends for the most part leave me to my own devices.
    Materially I have little.
    O Vierge des Pauvres, je vous remercie. J'ai voulu la pauvreté et elle m'embrase forcement. [O Virgin of the Poor, I thank you. I wanted poverty, and it embraces me fiercely.]
    Vierge, non, je ne te donne rien. Tu m'as fait cadeau de la pauvreté et de la souffrance [Virgin, no, I give you nothing. You have given me the gift of poverty and suffering] & by these two pearls I am ground into a host.
    O Mary, I dare not say I have nothing more to give or what remains (I do not know) will be torn from me as a limb.
    I renew—so deeply conscious of what I am, my weakness, my imperfection—the words of consecration: all I have and am—*oui! Vierge des Pauvres, oui, oui! Mais, O Mère, pitié, ego sum pauper et solus, et je suis si las.* [Virgin of the Poor, yes, yes! But O Mother, have pity, I am a beggar and alone, and I am so weary.] But I will risk all, all, all.
    O Vierge des Pauvres, ayez pitié de moi. Voyiez mes larmes—pitié, pitié, pitié. [O Virgin of the Poor, have pity on me. Look at my tears—have pity, have pity, have pity.][4]

He signed it "Aloysius Schwartz, *Pretre et Pauper*"—priest and beggar.

SHORTLY AFTER PENNING THE PRAYER, he returned to the Korean chancery, half-starved in appearance and besieged in body and spirit.

[4] PM.

In humiliation, he conceded that his return to America to recuperate was for the best. He had no money for his airfare; he had used it up attempting to restore his health—and in helping his troubled friend, the late Michael Rhi. Busan's bishop, John Choi, told Father Al he could not help finance his return home. From his old chancery bedroom, where cold winds blowing in from the Sea of Japan still made their way through window cracks to harass him, he prayed for resolve and a miracle.

Finally, someone told Father Al about a kindly American ship captain who had just unloaded his cargo at the Busan harbor. Begging free transportation home, he won over the captain's benevolence. In early 1959, he was the lone passenger on a humble tramp steamer, the *Robin S. Mowbray*, which was on a keeling course for a port outside of San Francisco. The journey was a low point for Father Al; he felt he had turned his back on his Korean family and God-appointed mission territory, and he didn't know when, or if, he'd be well enough to return. He rode out a torturously sea-sick voyage in a fog. "The ship, empty and top-heavy ... pitched, tossed, and rolled onward to the Golden Gate Bridge in San Francisco", he wrote. "[I would] wonder silently if the North Pacific would not be too much for our crazy, lopsided vessel."

Throughout his thirteen-day journey, he never even once paused to consider the treasure that he stuffed into his duffel bag before sailing: a handful of Polaroids he had taken of poverty-stricken Korea. Before his departure, he had borrowed a camera and casually snapped some photographs. Eventually these Polaroids would play a central role in Father Al's work, giving a face to the starved and silent of Korea. But now, Schwartz was a sick man, and was thinking only of getting well.

When the *Mowbray*'s gangway was finally lowered onto the firm land of California, Father Al was greeted by a heavyset, gregarious customs official whom he remembered years later as Mr. Murphy.

"What've you got in there, Father?" he asked, pointing to his duffel bag. "Gold or opium?"

"Both", replied Father Al, deadpan, wobbly-kneed, weak, and ghost-like in appearance.

Mr. Murphy brightened at the tired priest's droll sense of humor and immediately asked what he was doing for dinner. A few hours later his newest friend pulled up to a large house with a beautifully manicured lawn. Inside was a collection of elegantly arranged rooms that were exquisitely furnished. A meal of chicken, mashed potatoes, asparagus, salad, and ice cream and cake awaited them upon their arrival. As Mr. Murphy announced to his wife and three children that he was skipping dessert to honor his diet, Father Al was still absorbing the lightning bolt of reverse culture shock.

"[Busan] was still fresh in my memory", he remembered, "with its thousands of tents, shacks, and squatter huts, its teeming, squalid, overcrowded streets; [Busan] with its beggars, refugees, orphans, rag-pickers, dump-dwellers, and thousands of hungry people lining up at feeding stations each day. All this was fresh in my mind and it contrasted sharply with America, reseen and revisited after an absence."[5]

With a few hours to kill before Father Al's flight to Washington, D.C., Mr. Murphy asked him if he wanted to spend some time visiting with his pastor at his parish down the street. He said it was a ten-minute walk, and it struck Father Al as strange that Mr. Murphy walked toward his car to drive them there. *Comfort and convenience,* he must have thought as he stepped through the passenger-side door—*the American way.* At the church, Monsignor Smith (Father Al's pseudonym for him) threw the door open and after introductions began to pelt the missionary priest with questions about the state of Korea. After some time, the pastor offered his guest a tour of his brand-new rectory. "He pointed out its features and highlights, with all the subdued effervescence of a soft-sell real estate agent", Father Al later recalled. "Central air-conditioning. Wall-to-wall carpeting. Built-in TV for each room. Adjustable lounge chairs. Indirect lighting and wood paneling throughout." Monsignor Smith finished the tour in front of a large wooden cabinet with a wide array of bottles and glasses. "What'll it be, pal?" Father Al remembered him asking. "Scotch or bourbon?"[6]

Already in his first day back in the States, he was being introduced to startling contrasts that stopped him in his tracks. It would become the persistent thorn of his homecoming. Monsignor Smith showed off the wood paneling, and Father Al thought about mud walls. Smith talked about a modernized, comfortable home, and Father Al stayed

[5] *StSi,* 92.
[6] *StSi,* 94.

in quiet thought about Michael and the garbage-dump neurotics in the mountain hovels built over sewage.

When he finally made it back to Washington, D.C., he spent a few months of pleasant convalescence in his father's small Channing Street row home. Father Al then considered himself well enough to begin to attempt to raise awareness of and donations for the Korean poor. His humble campaign, however, started with what may have seemed a slap to the face. Citing the financial needs of the poor in his own diocese, Washington Archbishop Patrick O'Boyle barred Father Al from seeking donations within his home diocese. After receiving the unsettling news, Father Al began hitchhiking and purchasing bus fares to homes, schools, parishes, and religious centers outside of the area. On these trips, he discovered that his photographs from Korea gripped people powerfully. Father Al saw the look in their eyes as they absorbed the dire consequences of the human toll of war. He had grown so accustomed to the poverty of his Korean surroundings that he didn't anticipate how impactful the images would be to others. The photos proved so moving, in fact, that he converted them into a short slideshow. After some time, money started to come, enough that he was able to purchase a used black Renault Dauphine, one of the tiniest cars on the road at the time. Thereafter, he began driving his mini-mobile to various places down the eastern seaboard of America, begging for the Korean poor. Eight months of work netted twenty-seven thousand dollars, which he deposited in Bishop Choi's First National Bank account in New York City. When Father Al had told Murphy in San Francisco that he was carrying gold in his bag, he was halfway right.

When he felt the solo begging tour beginning to take a bodily toll, he headed back to Washington. A few days later, he left for an extended retreat at a Trappist monastery buried in Virginia farmland. One night, as he was quietly washing the dinner dishes of his fellow retreatants, a gentleman with indomitable energy named Gratian Meyer approached and offered to help dry and put away the dinnerware. A gregarious sort, Gratian struck up a conversation and asked Father Al what brought him to the Trappists. As Father Al began to speak, Meyer was held spellbound. When the dishes were put away, the pair sat down and spoke well into the night. In the course of their conversation, Father Al explained that he hoped to return to

Korea within the year, where he would remain, hopefully, forever. He mentioned that the Trappist retreat was serving as a respite and small reward for the donations he had been able to scrape up on his recently completed road trip. Gratian's interest was piqued; he asked Father Al how much he had collected, and the sum rang unimpressively to Meyer. The former World War II fighter pilot and owner of a direct mail and marketing company looked the priest in the eye. "Father," he said, "I think I can really help you."[7]

In a meeting shortly after the retreat at a downtown office in Washington, Gratian told Father Al that the future of direct-mail fundraising involved what he called "premiums", which were inserted into appeal letters. He explained that Father Al's mailed appeals for donations should include an inexpensive rosary, or a photograph of a Korean child, or religious stamps, or a prayer card of a Korean martyr, or some such memento. Father Al rolled his eyes, but Gratian showed him the results he'd helped other firms achieve through similar approaches. Still, Father Al considered the premiums distasteful; he had seen his own results through the power of storytelling.

Gratian convinced Father Al to permit him to orchestrate a small trial run. Within a month, a steady stream of donations began to filter in. Gratian extended his mailing list, and Bishop Choi's First National Bank account continued to grow. The poor of Busan, Korea, were slowly being fed.

Thanks to this fundraising adaptation, Korean Relief, Inc., was born. It was Lent 1961. Father Al was thirty years old, and he hadn't the foggiest idea of what he had begun. By 1964, a hodgepodge of entertainers, athletes, and celebrities had signed on to become sponsors and supporters of Korean Relief: Bing Crosby, Roger Staubach, Willie Stargell, Efrem Zimbalist, Jr., Jonas Salk, M.D., Phyllis Diller, Harvey Korman, Ed McMahon, Mamie Eisenhower, and Mrs. Joseph Kennedy all joined with Father Al—along with many tens of thousands of other donors.[8]

Heartened by the early success, Bishop Choi—who had grown up poor in the Korean countryside and had never set foot outside of his Busan diocese—arrived in Washington in April of 1961 to assist

[7] PM.
[8] PM.

Father Al in raising funds. He was wearing a pair of high-heeled boots. When after a week Father Al hesitatingly inquired about his footwear, his Excellency explained that he couldn't afford to buy a pair of shoes for himself. The dress shoes were given to him as a gift by an order of nuns. Father Al considered that either he didn't know his shoes were meant for women or he simply didn't care. When it was finally suggested that he considered purchasing a new pair of shoes, Bishop Choi instead cut off half of the high heels.

After spending some time getting to know Father Al's family and touring the nation's capital, the pair hopped into the priest's Renault Dauphine and began their six-month begging tour. They ended up visiting more than fifty parishes, as far west as Minneapolis, as far north as Montreal, and as far south as Mexico City. Choi was astounded by the generosity of American Catholics, who responded in full to his soft-spoken pleas for money. Father Al wrote in his journals what his bishop shared about his experience in the US: "I am a little bishop from a little country. What is more, I am a foreigner and a stranger. America is a big and powerful nation and when I first came here I was afraid that I would not be treated well." He continued: "Wherever I went, however, I was not treated as a little bishop from a little country, nor as a foreigner or a stranger. I was treated as a bishop of the Catholic Church. Everywhere—in convents, rectories and homes of individual Catholics—I was received with the same respect and reverence that Americans show their own bishops. Truly this is a sign of the deep faith of American Catholics in the universality of the Church."[9]

As the pair traveled America's back roads on behalf of Busan's poor—spending their nights in rectories, seminaries, monasteries, and the homes of the laity—Father Al explained to his bishop his hunger to return to what he felt was his God-appointed mission territory. The one-man Korean Relief office back in Washington, Father Al explained, was fully functional on its own and managing the steady flow of donations. There was no longer a pressing need for his presence in America. Bishop Choi disagreed, advising instead that Father Al consider continuing his work as a fundraiser in America; he cited the wonders of what God was accomplishing for the

[9] PM.

poor through US-based direct mailing. The back-and-forth discussions continued. Finally, at the end of their travels, Father Al had had enough. He related in his journal what he said to Choi: "'Bishop, I have been ordained three years now. Half of that time I was sick, the other half I was raising money. Is this what I was ordained for? Please, I want to go back to Korea and stay!' He looked at me in surprise and reluctantly agreed. So, I had another lease on life and I returned to Korea."[10]

En route to Korea the autumn of 1961, Father Al agreed to travel to Europe to team up, once again, with Bishop Choi, where together they begged for their last bit of charity. The pair landed safely home together in Seoul just before Christmas. When Bishop Choi offered Mass at Busan's cathedral on Christmas morning, he based his homily on the immensity of God's power shown through the generosity of the American people. In the midst of sharing stories from the road, he broke down in tears. Within seconds, a sizable amount of Mass-goers also fell into tears; so many of them were the beneficiaries of the begging tour's fruits. Father Al was awestruck. For the first time, he paid witness to the power of Korean Relief. He started to piece things together in his mind; his extended time of physical travail and loneliness may have been God's plan all along.

FATHER AL WAS APPOINTED A PASTOR at one of the poorest parishes in the diocese, Song-do Catholic Church, which was situated in a small village by Cheonma Mountain. The majority of his parishioners arrived for Mass unshowered and lived in tar-papered shanties or, as he discovered, in abandoned Japanese tombs. Some washed their clothes in gutters that captured the release of the dirty water from public bath houses. No longer was he a sightseeing connoisseur of the poverty-stricken; he was a priest caught up within the fly-infested middle of it. He sought the help of three Korean Benedictine nuns to breathe life into the battered but hardy souls of his parish. Because the language barrier remained immense, he reached out once again to his old friend, Damiano Park—his "Korean Man Friday" as Father Al called him—to become the fourth full-time parish employee. Damiano would spend up to five hours a day,

[10] PM.

in the early mornings or late at night, working to help Father Al learn the Korean language.

It was a happy period in his priesthood where every day seemed a consolation. He felt, finally, like he was beginning to enter into the lives of the people he served, as a father to their souls; he was hearing many confessions, spending time with his parishioners in their small homes, helping to feed the poor, and walking the neighborhood, praying the Rosary, and smiling at passersby. He was a priest well-loved by his community, like the revered Abbé Duggot, with whom he'd spent a summer in the French village of Bauduen. He felt singularly blessed, but he also began to wonder whether obliging his daily priestly tasks was becoming too pleasant, or even too *easy*. Images of Sister Melfrieda's comfortable convent in the slums and the Maryknolls' middle-ground approach tweaked his conscience.

In 1962, without a word to anyone, he gave Damiano a set of keys to his humbly constructed cinder-block rectory and moved into a shack that stood pitifully at the base of a mountain in the rear of the rectory. Although he had not professed a vow of poverty, his priesthood from the very beginning was clothed in it, which was why his new home—which wasn't even fit for a prisoner—made sense to him. Some townsfolk mistook it for an outhouse. It lacked electricity, running water, and plumbing, with a tar-papered roof that was caving in in places. But it was, he thought, where Christ would have lived. The interior walls of his new one-room home were made of hardened mud, and his weather-beaten and leaky outhouse, narrower than a telephone booth, was set up twenty-five feet from his front door. He knew his living quarters lacked all decorum, but it was one where he could make a deeper impression on those who lived in the tombs; it was a home where his destitute parishioners would find comfort sharing a cup of tea with him.

He described what villagers began calling "the pastor's poorhouse" in his private writings:

> The place looked very uninviting and I wasn't sure whether it was livable or not. I turned to Damiano and asked what he thought. His reply was simply: "Sure, Father, with determination you can do it." That simple remark was decisive and I decided, under the circumstances, to give it a try....

I fixed up the shack as best I could and moved in. It worked, but just barely. I encountered a number of difficulties. First was the smell, a rich, earthy, overpowering, Korean smell, composed of human excrement, dead animals, garbage, bugs, and dirt. At first the smell was so awful I had trouble sleeping at night. But I kept shifting my sleeping bag about the house until I eventually found a corner where the air was somewhat breathable. Then I made a determined assault to extricate the cause of the odor. I discovered one or two rodents in the walls, and using some chemicals eventually changed the odorous aspect of the parish house. Also, I am sure that unconsciously my sensitive American nose became desensitized with time, and although the smell lingered on, my reaction to it diminished.

The smell from the dead rats was one problem. The noise at night from the live rats which scurried about in the space between the roof and the ceiling was another problem. Korean rats are real swingers, and every night when I lay down to sleep, they would come alive and start a disco dance just over my head. Before crawling into my bed at night, I would position a broom alongside me. When the rats got too exuberant, I would hit the ceiling with a broom. This would startle them into immobility for a period of time. I waged constant warfare with the rats and although at times I seemed to be winning, I guess the final result would best be termed a "stand-off."

Another problem was the cold. During winter months cold, icy winds would find their way through many cracks, holes, and crevices, and at times, heating the place properly became something of a problem. The shack was heated by yonthen coal as are most homes in Korea. Yonthen coal briquettes are made of compressed coal dust and clay. They heat the floor from below and this works pretty good except they give off a deadly, odorless carbon monoxide gas which every year claims many lives in Korea. While living in my "poorhouse," on two or three occasions when the floor cracked, or at night when the air was laden and heavy and prevented the smoke from exiting properly, the cottage became filled with yonthen fumes. Several times, I remember stumbling out the front door semi-conscious, and reeling as a drunkard leaving a tavern at night. After a while, I considered the yonthen too dangerous and eventually installed a small diesel-burning space heater. One night I woke up to find my shack on fire as a result of the diesel fuel leaking, but the fire was quickly put out and there was very little damage.

Such were the perils of trying to live the poor life in Korea. But poor-style living had its positive elements as well. One's surroundings definitely condition one's thinking. By living more or less poor, I discovered that it was much easier to think poor, to feel poor, and to stay on the same wavelength as the poor.[11]

Father Al didn't want anyone to know he lived like this. Whenever anyone inquired about his welfare or the state of his mountainside shack, he deflected the topic and cheerfully poked fun at himself. Throughout the five years of living there, he presented himself to his parishioners and the poor he served as the happiest missionary in the world. He told everyone about the uncatchable "bandit" that stole his roll of toilet paper from his outhouse each week. He didn't tell anyone, though, that the bleakness of the shack had become for him a remarkable paradox; it had managed to warm his soul and invite him more deeply than ever before into an embrace of the Holy Trinity. He felt that when he prayed the Office in the darkness of the shack, he was being suffused into the eternal chorus of suffering saints. It was the Spanish mystic John of the Cross to whom he drew closest. He shared in a letter to his spiritual companion Sister Gertrude, "I find great comfort in [John's] words, 'When the soul grasps its nothingness, it is ready for union.' "[12]

He heard that a number of nearby parish priests had begun to mock his chosen living conditions; they regarded it as a morbid and unnecessarily theatrical gesture of piety and asceticism. Whenever he was confronted by a member of the clergy about his radical decision to live like a poor man, he said he felt that God had called him there, for God is often most easily found in deserts. Some approached him to say he had made a spectacle of himself, which Father Al wondered about privately in his journal:

> [Perhaps] my lifestyle was a silent reproach to them. They found this difficult to accept. "Why don't you live like everybody else?" was a frequent question they threw at me. "What are you trying to prove?" "Why don't you live in a place where you can adequately work and function as a pastor?" Some priests called my house "the monkey cage." I had no intention of giving a lesson to anybody and I was somewhat embarrassed by these questions. However, I

[11] PM.
[12] DJ, 127.

thought the positive aspects outweighed the negative ones, and so I opted to continue.... My years in the "poorhouse" were ones of light and grace. And I look back upon this period of time with gratitude and nostalgia.[13]

In Father Al's book *Poverty: Sign of Our Times*—which he wrote a few years after his period in the shack—he described a "Father Jackson" who moved out of his rectory and into a run-down shanty. "This simple gesture on his part effectively served as a sign and a witness", he wrote. "It said something to both the people of the parish and the priests of the diocese. The people and the priests did not necessarily like what it said but this is another point.... [Father Jackson] tried to reason with them pointing out that Jesus himself lived in a stable and died on a cross stripped of all possessions."[14]

While not at work accomplishing the ordinary tasks of a parish priest, Father Al spent his free time in prayer, writing a book, *The Starved and the Silent*, and reading from the lives of the saints. He also carved out as many hours as he was able to master the Korean language with Damiano's help. One cold January morning, his tutor was startled by what Father Al quietly revealed to him. When the heat from a small charcoal stove began to make Damiano's feet itch, he drew his shoeless feet together and rubbed them against one another. The act became a distraction to Father Al. "I simply said that the stove heat makes my frozen feet itch", Damiano wrote. "Then, after a momentary silence, he removed a sock from one of his feet and showed me his foot. It was in the second stage of frostbite. I was stunned. I couldn't say a word. He put his sock back on and we resumed our study, without any further comment."[15]

Sister Michaela Kim, the handpicked successor of Father Al and the first superior general of the Sisters of Mary, remembered what it was like entering the American priest's shack for the first time. She thought it was "falling apart" and considered its darkness and bitter cold to be a remarkable austerity. "I truly wondered how he would survive in such a miserable condition", she said. "He was truly an example of poverty to us as well as to all priests and religious. He was

[13] PM.

[14] *Pov*, 78.

[15] Damiano Park, *Father Al Schwartz, Who Is Still Alive* (self-pub.), 27–28.

totally detached from worldly things. He had only very few clothes, furniture in his room, shoes, and books."[16]

Although the shack achieved its purpose of helping Father Al to conform to Christ the Poor Man, perhaps the greatest practical utility of his "poorhouse" was that it acted as an unassailable buffer. If administrators and clergy suspected him of abusing the tremendous amount of American money being mailed to Korean Relief, they could simply be led into his hovel. At the same time, his home served as a shield from more financially ambitious business people and Church leaders; after viewing his living conditions, they concluded that his cooperation in their ventures might be for naught.

When he moved into the shack in 1962, he didn't know that its four walls would become a winepress, crushing him, like Saint Paul, into a libation to be poured out in love. He would later tell the Sisters of Mary: "Mary realizes [the crucifix] is the heart and center of the Christian mystery, the heart and center of holiness—this crucifix— Christ nailed to the cross, and we, nailed to the cross with Christ.... Jesus again and again repeats this mystery on every page of the Gospel. 'Unless you renounce all that you possess—your health, your reputation, your material possessions, your pleasure, all your goods— you cannot be my disciple.' "[17]

[16] *Pos*, 138–39.
[17] Serm, 7:167–68.

8

Hard Road to a Miracle

Objections from Rome and the Founding of the Sisters of Mary,
1962–1964

OFTEN AT DUSK, passersby would see Father Al stealing the remains of
the day from the rocking chair on the porch outside of his shack. He'd
wave and smile his broad toothy grin. A book was usually in his lap.
The image of their pastor at leisure was pleasing to his poor parishioners. It signaled to them that all was well with the foreign priest they
were starting to love. Just as Father Al had worked to master French
and Latin at seminary in Louvain, his untiring work with Damiano to
overcome the Korean language barrier was beginning to pay off. By
the end of 1963, he was speaking about Christ in long, halting conversations in his parishioners' native dialect, and his Song-do parish
community treasured him for it. They saw their simple parish priest
as one having fully embraced their pre-Christian Confucian principles
of honor, harmony, and respect, principles that had been passed on
as sacred heirlooms through unnumbered generations. The poor saw
Father Al's commitment to enter fully among them; he had earned his
passport of acceptance. All the while, his choice to take up residence
in the shack indicated to those in the slums that he had *become* them.
They had never known anyone like him.

This five-year period of his priesthood was marked by graces and
close friendship with God; Father Al seemed to radiate joy everywhere he went. He often invited children and teens from the slums
to follow him up Cheonma Mountain and other hillsides, where he
spread out blankets for picnics and began to test his imperfect dialect
in conversations about their lives. As he sat on his porch at night, he

saw small campfires rising from these same slopes; he saw the faint light from hovels as flickering pinholes of hope. Children watched him dive into the frigid Sea of Japan to test his arms against the strength of heavy tides. He often swam up beside the small wooden boats of startled Korean fishermen, many of whom had never seen a person who wasn't their own countryman. When he was alone, he often sat on high cliff sides, where the mountains met the sea, and fell into long periods of contemplation about Christ's hidden life, the saints, and the priesthood. As Father Al stared into the waters, he knew he had "arrived" as a missionary priest. He was in the thick of things, and as he walked back down into the slums, he praised God for taking him to the very center of the life he'd dreamed about as a child.

From his rocking chair, Father Al read not only Church documents and Scripture, but also the biographies of contemplatives and saints. He saw the indwelling of Christ most powerfully in the ascetics, mystics, and martyrs, gravitating toward John of the Cross, Teresa of Avila, John Vianney, Charles de Foucauld, Damien of Molokai, Ignatius of Loyola, Francis de Sales, and Catherine of Siena. He wrote in these early days as a priest of being moved by Martin of Tours shearing his cape for the street beggar, by Foucauld launching out into the bleakness of the Algerian desert for the poor and the unbaptized, and by Francis of Assisi throwing off every degree of comfort to renounce his life for Christ. He articulated this severe method of forsakenness in the following way:

> In the psalms, the Holy Spirit says, and He is quoting God, "I dwell in a place which is dry and waterless." God dwells in the desert; He dwells in nothingness, emptiness, extreme poverty. If you want to find God, renounce all your possessions and seek God. Jesus died poor on the cross. He is stripped naked. He has no good reputation. He gives His mother. He is alone. His disciples have left Him, and He has no friends. The blood leaves His body—health and strength and life leave his body.... He empties Himself completely and the figure of Jesus on the cross is that of total, absolute, terrible, frightening poverty. Jesus says, "If you wish to be my disciple, you must renounce all that you possess." All means visible possessions and invisible possessions. What is on the outside, what is on the inside—all.[1]

[1] *Serm*, 9:5, 12.

As a thirty-two-year-old priest in 1962, he understood it was time for him to become like the poor. But even as the witness of lionhearted saints filtered up from the pages of his books to inspire and form his soul, it is certain that Father Al often felt utterly alone and experienced what might best be described as a downheartedness because of separation from his saintly heroes. He sensed he was dissimilar to all of the martyrs and holy souls, who had died and gained their eternal reward. Unlike them, this American missionary was the custodian of an enormous amount of money—a cross that perhaps pressed even harder into him than his marathon struggle with hepatitis had. Korean Relief's steady flow of money kept him constantly tethered to its custodianship.

Other than the four or five hours he slept each night and the time he spent reading on his porch, he filled each hour of the day with acts of charity, service to the poor, instruction to the ignorant, offering the sacraments, and all his other priestly duties. He was spending more and more time in state-run orphanages, hospitals, schools, leper colonies, and tubercular wards that were the beneficiaries of Korean Relief. And it was his visits to these places that began to harrow and change him. Too often he saw crushed souls. When he made eye contact, too often the eyes looking back at him were listless, sad, or seemingly caught up in a different dimension.

His visits to the orphanages were the hardest. Father Al saw that the children were joyless. The sustenance from Korean Relief helped to nourish their bodies, but their souls were starving in the abyss of the deplorable state wards. At best, public children's care in Korea was substandard and unjust, and at its worst, it was vulgar and demonic. The brutality of what he saw goaded his conscience: welts, lesions, and catatonic states. On walks back to his parish, he passed through alleyways scattered with dying and expressionless people, and the parable of the Good Samaritan repeatedly came to mind. On the spot, he did what he could to administer help, but the effects of war remained catastrophic in Busan. Rather than diminishing with time, poverty and despair had become embedded into its people trapped by neglect and grief. As he moved from place to place, the heartening parable of the Good Samaritan transitioned into a haunting record that spun accusatorially within his head. Like the Samaritan, he wanted to grab hold of the broken man, place him on a donkey, and bring him to an inn. But in a city stained by war and destitution, too many of Busan's innkeepers were uncaring and corrupt. And he knew there were tens of thousands who needed saving.

In the darkness of his shack, an invisible hand led him to a life-changing recognition: *he* was to become the innkeeper of the parable.

At night, on the front porch, as Father Al rocked in his second-hand chair to the sounds of the Korean night, he understood that it was God who, in his permissive will, paradoxically prescribed his long illness, as well as the contradictory medicine of desperation, iso-lation, and physical pain—trials so unrelenting that they had sent him home to America in humiliation. He didn't consider his Stateside encounter with Gratian Meyer as happenstance. God had put the convivial direct-mailing expert beside him, dish towel in hand. It was Meyer who helped ignite the engine of Korean Relief, and Father Al knew that God would drive it forward. Humbly, the priest acknowl-edged that he had been called, simply, to be its steward. Though the fundraising campaign had reaped an abundant harvest, the problem he faced was greater than money. Each day he walked through what seemed vast wastelands of people who felt forsaken by God. Korea itself needed resurrection.

IN AMERICA, a handful of bishops had become unnerved by the sub-stantial amount of money being directed halfway across the world to Korean Relief. They wrote a letter complaining to the Vatican that Korean Relief was encroaching upon their terrain by diverting funds from their own diocesan ministries for the poor. The bishops requested a complete stop to the nonprofit's solicitations in America.

Not long after, in 1962, Bishop Choi received a letter from Gre-gorio Cardinal Agagianian, the Vatican's prefect of the Sacred Con-gregation of the Propagation of the Faith, who was twice considered a serious papal candidate.[2] Agagianian detailed the concerns of the American bishops and requested that Father Al begin to pare back all of Korean Relief's solicitations in the United States. The priest and bishop both read the letter in disbelief. They had been eyewitnesses to all that America's generosity had done to begin to alleviate the

---

[2] Many thought it would be Agagianian, not Angelo Roncalli—the future Pope John XXIII—who would be elected pope by the College of Cardinals in 1958.

weight of poverty in war-torn Busan. They regarded the few US bishops' complaints as shortsighted, a dismissal of God's call to raise up the lowly from the dust and lift the needy from the ash heap (Ps 113:7). It was a casting off of a whole population they neither knew nor would ever see. Thinking of the parable of the Good Samaritan, Father Al considered the American bishops' posture comparable to that of the Levite and the priest who walked past the dying man because he wasn't one of them, because *he didn't look like them.*

Bishop Choi and Father Al agreed to take their dismay to prayer until a solution and proper response to Cardinal Agagianian came to them. Since they knew what the dire consequences would be for a Korean Relief program void of American donors, they agreed to continue operations in the meantime.

"[The American bishops] figured I was working their side of the street", Father Al wrote in his journals. "I was given no indication from Rome who the complaining bishops in the United States were, nor exactly what was the nature of their complaint. Nor did the United States bishops ever call me to inquire whether the program I had started was actually serving the poor, or doing something really effective in the cause of charity and justice."

He went on: "In other words, there seemed to be no consideration for the poor. The prime consideration was a bureaucratic, self-centered one. Also, in Rome, there was no desire, or even interest to determine if anything good or worthwhile was being accomplished on behalf of the downtrodden. The only concern centered on the fact that Church authorities in the United States were unhappy. Therefore, Church authorities in Rome were unhappy as well."[3]

Two months after the first letter, a sharply worded telegram arrived from the Vatican. Agagianian had been tipped off that the solicitation letters hadn't stopped. A more severe cease-and-desist order was issued, which prompted Bishop Choi to ask Father Al to fly to Rome and plead his case for the Korean poor. Although he understood the necessity of taking the trip, he was torn about whether he should go. The managerial demands of Korean Relief had become for him a hardship. When, at St. Charles College, the missionary hero Father Byrne set him on a path as a priest in a foreign land, he of

[3] PM.

course never considered running a nonprofit. Again as a Maryknoll, he detested the fact that formators were steering him away from the mission field toward an academic or administrative role. Now the administration of Korean Relief was stripping away so much time from his priestly and missionary duties, and he considered folding the program. But as he spent time praying about the trip, it began to become clear: "There was an impulse in me which urged me to do my best to keep it going."[4] Torn between obedience to his own bishop and obedience to a senior Vatican cardinal, he went to God Himself, with his demand that Father Al become the innkeeper. Father Al had vowed to die to help save the poor, and he knew that part of that death was accepting the undesired burden of his stewardship of Korean Relief. When he became resolved to travel to the Vatican, he began to strategize for his meeting with the unknown, high-powered cardinal.

Before departing, he visited a Carmelite monastery to speak to his friend Sister Gertrude, sharing his disillusionment with American bishops and his apprehension about the trip. Sister Gertrude, who had arrived in Korea in 1955, two years prior to Father Al, had grown extraordinarily close to the young priest shortly after their first encounter a few years earlier. No one would ever come to know the young priest's hidden struggles, inner workings of the soul, joys, and travails as well as this nun would, whom he regarded as his spiritual mother. Years later, in the days before he died, Father Al recollected the manner in which Sister Gertrude had spent the entirety of his time in Rome in prayer and fasting for the success of his confrontation against Cardinal Agagianian for the poor.

There is no written account of Cardinal Agagianian and Father Al's discussion, but it is clear that the cardinal was moved by the sincerity and frank simplicity of the young missionary, and by his devotion to the Korean poor. It is known that Father Al walked him through the story of Korean Relief's birth. He spoke of his illness, his return to America, of the early hitchhiking begging tours and his providential encounter with Gratian Meyer. He brought with him Korean Relief's founding documents and paperwork to indicate its legality. After a great deal of listening to what must have seemed

[4] *KMS*, 139.

to him convincing arguments, the cardinal revealed to a pleasantly startled Father Al that he had shown great prudence in refusing his cease-and-desist order; it evidenced the intensity of his love for those in Busan who were voiceless. Instead of a decisive reproof for disobedience—the thing he feared most—he was met with a wink and a nudge to carry on with his sacred work for the poor. Thereafter, their conversation centered on all that Father Al had in mind for helping to heal Korea's most vulnerable.

So moved was Cardinal Agagianian by Father Al's fight for the poor and his love for the priesthood that he gave him the parting gift of a giant golden ciborium. "It was so big, it reminded me of the Wimbledon Cup", Father Al said. "So, I returned to Busan in triumph, holding the ciborium above my head in two hands and presenting it to a chuckling and gleeful Bishop Choi."

But the news he carried was even better. "The Cardinal said there would be no more interference from him. In other words, he was willing to close his eyes to my little operation and I obtained a temporary stay of execution", he wrote in his journals.[5]

He claimed the confrontation had been won by Sister Gertrude, who he felt the Church should canonize. "I could write a book about my impossible mission to Rome. I felt like I was walking a tightrope which stretched from Korea to the Holy City, to the U.S. and then back to Korea and there was no safety net under the tightrope", Father Al confessed. "At every step of the way, I was at risk, one false move and everything would have been lost." He continued: "However, I felt I was being guided by a clear wisdom and I was being helped by an invisible power. When I returned to Busan, Saint Sister Gertrude told me she had been praying for the success of my first mission, day and night. So, she was the one who achieved this first victory.... There was a spiritual faith which united us in our hearts. We were one in Jesus."[6]

In the ensuing year, when a handful of American bishops continued sending letters of complaint, Father Al decided to move his base of operations from Washington, D.C., to an old wedding hall in Busan, where the might of Korean Relief grew even stronger. With

[5] KMS, 140.
[6] KMS, 139-40.

its success, he instinctively understood that things had to change in his life. To remain perfectly obedient to God, he knew an interior mortification would have to take place; he would need to die to the missionary life he had always wanted.

Korean Relief had expanded into something far greater than anything he could have imagined, and with sober eyes he knew it was time to put the axe to the root of his role as a parish priest. Ever since the days he was known to classmates as "Little Mouse", he had simply wanted to love the poor, administer the sacraments, and spread the Gospel as a parish priest in a foreign land. It was part of the air he breathed. He had always known that the most authentic path to a priestly victimhood was one that mandated an unreserved availability to serve those darkened by poverty. It is what he strove for each day as a pastor. But he had come to see that, paradoxically, this wasn't the narrow path that God desired from him. God wanted a broader road, one that could accommodate his numberless thousands of disregarded. Father Al's access to large amounts of money could help the poor in a more wide-sweeping way than his one-on-one encounters. As much as he hated the thought, he knew the God-given flow of donations from Korean Relief was more powerful than his desire to serve the poor on a person-to-person basis.

Father Al's dilemma now was that to begin his new, all-encompassing mission, he needed not hundreds of thousands of dollars, but *millions*. After Gratian Meyer had introduced the need to include small gifts as part of his appeal letters, Father Al saw the success that prayer cards, stamps, small photographs, and other small "premiums" had in raising funds. But his vision to aid Busan's welfare system required deeper thought. Then an idea sparked to life—"Operation Hanky".

Father Al employed more than two thousand women to hand-stitch unique Asian designs, known as *tongyangsu*, on handkerchiefs to be included with his appeal letters. The challenging stitchwork featured whimsical scenes: children on teeter-totters, walking hand-in-hand, playing games, or reading from books. Father Al had a sense that Americans would be impacted by the "old-fashioned, amateurish approach" of hand-embroidered artwork. He also knew that Americans would have no idea that the single mothers, war widows, paralytics, and housewives who stitched them—not to mention the high-school-aged girls who handwrote the names and addresses on the appeal envelopes—were some of the poorest individuals in the world.

Within a few months, tens of thousands of new American donors had been won over by the embroidery and Father Al's accompanying tales from the streets of Busan. Donations from every state began to pour in. In 1964, two years after the start of Operation Hanky, Korean Relief's donor list had swelled to more than a half million, which meant that in the span of two years approximately five hundred thousand handkerchiefs had left Korea in solicitation envelopes. After completing a comprehensive study, Father Al determined that ninety-eight percent of donations went directly to the poor, even though he still managed to pay each employee a wage that was sixty percent higher than that of everyday Korean factory workers. At the height of the campaign, more than 3,500 Koreans were receiving a steady paycheck for their labor that spread into four different parts of Busan.

Seemingly overnight, Korean Relief, Inc., had become one of the largest relief services in the world. Father Al was thirty-four years old. He wrote in a letter to a close friend: "[God] does not want me to dig a hole in the field, bury it and sit on it. He wants me to use [money from donations] effectively, thereby generating more grace and giving him pleasure and glory."[7]

IT WAS AROUND THIS TIME that he was led more intensely to a particular figure: the Frenchman Saint Vincent de Paul. Praying and rocking on his chair beneath the deep blue night, he turned over images of de Paul and the Virgin of the Poor in his head—and another idea came.

Father Al shared a good deal in common with Vincent de Paul. Vincent was a priest who hungered to live among the poor but also had access to vast reservoirs of money. In the early seventeenth century, he had worked as a chaplain in a number of rich and noble households, including the French Royal Court, but he was happiest as a poor parish priest. One wealthy woman, the Countess de Gondi, understood his sense of poverty and encouraged him to work with the hard-up, uncatechized French peasantry in her lands. Bankrolling his projects, she had him establish a community

[7] *DJ*, x.

of missionaries to teach the poor, which was immensely successful. De Paul would go on to collaborate with wealthy patrons for the rest of his life, building massive organizations and structures for charitable services—the first of their kind in Europe. (In fact, the very term "charity" as a description of an institute for merciful works comes from de Paul, whose network was nicknamed "*La Charité*".[8]) Father Al saw in Saint Vincent an authentic Christian model for using wealth to lift up the needy.

Perhaps more importantly, though, Vincent de Paul sparked Father Al's sense of the power of collaboration. De Paul saw the overwhelming need for great numbers of volunteers to help distribute food and bring warmth and Christian instruction to the poor. In Louise de Marillac, a bright young widow and mother hoping to give her life to God, he encountered a dynamo who could help him meet the demands of caring for hundreds of thousands of peasants, prisoners, orphans, and infirm. Noting her boundless energy, organizational skills, and devotion to the Catholic faith, Vincent asked Louise to begin to educate young, humble country women on ways to serve the poor effectively.[9] These peasant women would become the Daughters of Charity, an army of consecrated women who would spread throughout France and beyond. After they were trained and catechized, these nuns of simple stock went to orphanages, prisons, hospitals, schools, mental institutions, and battlefields and into the far-flung homes of those worn down by poverty and isolation. By the mid-seventeenth century, hundreds of thousands of the poor throughout France—eventually, throughout Europe—were being helped by the heroic work of the Daughters of Charity.[10]

For Father Al, the background of these women was key. Nuns raised in poverty, he knew, would grasp its brutality more keenly than university-educated nuns. Holiness was not absorbed mainly through dissertations and classroom theory, but through doing and dying to oneself. Moreover, one born into poverty would be more eager to serve the people she saw as her own.

---

[8] Antonio Sicari, *Il grande libro di ritratti di santi* (Milan: Jaca Book, 1997), 307ff.

[9] Sicari, *Il grande libro*, 327ff.

[10] "Daughters of Charity of Saint Vincent de Paul," Encyclopedia Britannica, last accessed February 3, 2021, https://www.britannica.com/topic/Daughters-of-Charity-of -Saint-Vincent-de-Paul.

With de Paul and de Marillac's approach in mind—and thinking, too, of his old hero Saint John Bosco, the rescuer of children—Father Al decided to fix his gaze on the lonely, traumatized street urchins of Korea, whose vacant stares had haunted him since his first day in Seoul. By the end of the Korean War, there were more than one hundred thousand orphans in South Korea, and it was time to do something for them. In seminary, Father Al had begun to warm to Bosco, who had worked tirelessly to redirect the lives of Italian street children, juvenile delinquents, and orphans by encouraging them to stay active and pure through sports, devoted prayer lives, and physical and mental work. Father Al had taken a similarly integrated approach with the deceased Michael Rhi and some other Korean orphans with whom he had established friendships. But he knew there were tens of thousands of more Michaels that were beyond his reach. He wanted to get each of them and would begin to try. But he would not do it alone. Using the money of his donors, he would found an order, made up of the poor native daughters of Korea.

"He was a modern-day John Bosco who left everything for the poor", Monsignor Golasinski said. "But more importantly, he modeled everything after de Paul. He knew what the saint did about the power of de Marillac and holy women."

FATHER AL PLACED an advertisement in Korea's largest Catholic weekly newspaper, requesting the immediate assistance of young women willing to dedicate their lives in service to orphans and the indigent. Within a week, his mailbox began to fill with responses from across the country. He sensed the letters he was opening were signed by a population of young women who, whether they said it or not, wanted to live as nuns on fire with charity. Yet he was honest with them. When interviewees came, he told them they would have to awaken early each morning brimming with energy to rub life back into the souls of street children and orphans. The vast, Dickensian institutions he had so often visited had come to haunt him, and he emphasized that working in his orphanages would require a stiff repudiation of soulless government care. He was blunt about the form this would take: a devotedness to prayer and abnegation, a grinding work ethic, a strong backbone, and most importantly a desire to become a servant. They would be Martha as much as Mary.

He promised the women, though, that their service would stir in them a joy they had never known.

The majority of the applicants were daughters of poor families. There was a modesty in their bearing. They didn't dress up for the interviews, but came as they were. And one after the other, Father Al saw in them a willingness and determination to oblige his strict model of Christ-like sacrifice. By listening to their stories, he gained an understanding of the obstacles they had overcome and of the many wounds they still carried. He sensed, though, that the work of removing orphans' wounds would help to heal their own. He had found his first small brigade of de Marillacs.

And so the *Mariahwe*—in English, the "Sisters of Mary"—was born, under the patronage of the Virgin of the Poor. The day was August 15, 1964, the Feast of the Assumption. Father Al wrote to one friend explaining his reason for starting the order, which was initially called the *Maria Pomohwe* (the "Maria Orphan-Mother Society"): "[It was] founded to seek out and serve not just the poor, but the poorest of the most destitute, and those most lowly."[11] Twelve women were chosen, all in their twenties. They would join him in caring for the beloved poor Mary had visited at Banneux.

---

[11] *Pos*, 380.

9

Explosion of Grace

The Mission of the Sisters, 1964–1969

FATHER AL'S INSTRUCTIONS to the new sisters of the Mariahwe were simple: Try your best. Offer to Jesus even the littlest things you do for the children. A photograph of the twelve postulants taken shortly after joining the congregation reveals what look to be eager and joy-filled university students, though they were almost all unschooled.

"When he started it all, he knew he didn't want overly educated women helping him with the work", Monsignor Golasinski recalled. "Confucianism in Korea has always put a stress on schooling and education, but Father Al didn't want or need that. As soon as a young lady would enter the Mariahwe and Father Al saw the makings of holiness, he didn't spend much time with her novitiate; he was hoping she would dive right in to help the poor."

Golasinski went on: "It was his thought that too much education separated nuns from the heart of the poor they served—and he was right. Overseas in America, thousands of educated and habited nuns were just beginning to drop out of convents. A mutation had taken place in convents after Vatican II, something far different from how beautifully nuns were portrayed in [the 1945 film] *The Bells of St. Mary's*. Father Al gravitated toward simple and joy-filled nuns."

Because he was still inundated by his day-to-day parish duties, service throughout the diocese, and management of Korean Relief, Father Al sought the assistance of two faithful Benedictine nuns, Sister Helena and Sister Sophia, to help form the women in Scripture, catechesis, and child psychology, as well as in the management of orphanages.

But these were not run-of-the-mill orphanages. Because Father
Al knew that parentless children thirsted for family life, he established what he called small "family units", with a hundred or so small
children divided up among various cottages near his Song-do parish. Each of the twelve young women would act as a benevolent
"mother" to seven or eight children per home. In these intimate and
tender settings, Father Al knew, grace could break through, and the
slow process of healing could begin.

Although Schwartz himself never expressed the connection, the
homeland Father Al wanted to create for orphans may be imaged
by the ancient port city of Ephesus, where Saint John the Apostle and the Virgin Mary are believed to have settled in the years
after Christ's Ascension. This city on the Aegean Sea, in present-day
Turkey, was populated in part with retired Roman centurions, who
had been awarded large plots of land that overlooked the water and
sun-splashed mountains. With its Mediterranean climate, Ephesus
boasted well-tended valleys of wheat, proportioned rows of grape
vines, broom-swept porches, and tidy and well-kept homes—an
order that took on a new spiritual dimension when the Christian faith
entered. In his letter to the community, Paul commended the families of Ephesus for their great fraternal love: "Because I have heard
of your faith in the Lord Jesus and your love toward all the saints, I
do not cease to give thanks for you" (Eph 1:15–16). With John and
Mary living in their midst, we can imagine that these Christian families had firsthand stories of the life, death, and resurrection of Jesus
of Nazareth.

Father Al, not unlike Saint John Bosco, wanted this type of tran-
quility and order within his new communities. On the one hand,
pain-darkened souls, further scarred by indifference and bad care,
could taste resurrection only through a constant irradiation of love.
But on the other hand, these orphans also required something they
had never known: a form, a structure. Father Al knew this, and he
wanted children to experience how basic order can lay the foundation for a restful and strife-free life. The missionary priest knew the
harmony that family, assigned chores, play time, sports, three square
meals, an education, devoted prayer, and a warm bed at night could
elicit in the children. He trusted that the young, cheery-faced religious sisters would give this to them. Father Al hoped that even if the

faith did not fully take root, this human radiance would stoke a flame in the children, which they could bring back into their communities in Busan and beyond.

Father Al often pointed the Sisters of Mary to the radicality of John Bosco's love as an example for which to strive. He regarded the Italian saint as a supernatural force of rescuing grace for children grasping for a hero. Bosco stepped in to help delinquent children when no one else would, and he even, as Father Al explained to the Sisters, took on the children's physical, mental, and emotional scars:

> While he was walking through the dormitory at night, if he could see a child who had a headache or a toothache, he would pray for him and his prayer would be in the spirit of Christ. He would ask God to take the headache from this boy and give it to him; to take the toothache from this youngster and give it to him. The boy's head would stop throbbing and Don Bosco would have a terrible headache; the boy's jaw would cease to swell and Don Bosco's jaw would begin to swell with a horrible toothache. This is in the spirit of the service of Christ.
>
> So, we are to serve in this manner. Here, you have the opportunity every day, all day, to sacrifice little things. You can accept these opportunities to sacrifice or you can reject them. Nobody will know. It is hidden.... However, if you really want to live your vocation and to produce results and experience this satisfaction which comes from serving in the name of Christ, you must develop the habit of sacrifice.[1]

FATHER AL USED DONATIONS from Operation Hanky to purchase some cheap land: a cesspool on a mountain, formerly used as a dumping ground for human waste and debris. After paying to have the contaminated soil drained, sterilized, and made safe by city workers, he built and opened the first of his many free medical dispensaries. He hired a doctor and a small team of nurses, joined by a handful of Sisters of Mary, to serve at a small concrete structure that stood humbly between the two largest slums in Busan. Within a week, as Father Al wrote in his journals, well over one hundred patients a day were climbing or being carried up the mountain for treatment. Not long after, he opened and staffed three more slum dispensaries.

[1] *Serm*, 9:237–38.

Within a year of founding the Mariahwe, overcrowded orphanages from all over Busan wanted to release children into the Sisters' care. And once again, Father Al knew he had to start thinking differently. He had to think bigger. "As time went on, he just kept morphing and morphing and morphing", Monsignor Golasinski said. "He just kept changing and growing and moving on to where the abandoned were. Since he was a fourteen-year-old boy, he knew what he wanted to do for the poor. And he was as bold about finding ways to do it as anyone I ever knew." Golasinski continued: "He was an innovator, and he went where no one else went for the poor. When he saw a challenge, he responded to it instantly. If something needed to be addressed as it regarded the poor, he addressed it. When I became his partner in the work [in the 1970s], I knew that everything he did for the poor was going to have success, because he was going to fight to make it so."

By 1967, he had built a hospital, a "beggars' hospice", a boys' technical school, a middle school for five hundred students in the slums, and two retirement homes for the homeless and aged. His religious congregation was serving at each of the sites, and although they were growing, they were stretched thin by the immensity of the needs of the poor in Busan. "There is so much to do over here, so few to do it, and so little to do it with, that at times one is tempted to become discouraged", Father Al reflected. "Still, one takes solace in the thought that God helps people one at a time, as individuals.... Our family-unit orphanage program will not take care of all the tens of thousands of orphans in Korea. But it will help a significant few, and this is what counts. It is a step, and this is infinitely better than standing idly by gnashing one's teeth and rending one's garments."[2]

The Sisters of Mary had become the most identifiable set of individuals in all of Busan. The congregation, which consisted almost entirely of women under the age of thirty-five, wore simple white rubber shoes and dressed in plain black dresses with white collars. Rather than living in a more traditional convent, the Sisters of Mary's aspirants, postulants, novices, and professed sisters lived in an assortment of tiny homes where they slept on mats and prayed in a chapel

[2] *StSi*, 153.

without pews, kneelers, or chairs. After a full year of training, novices made promises of poverty, chastity, obedience, and lifelong dedication to serve the poor. They spent three hours of each day in prayer and the remainder in service. They often had smiling young orphans strapped to their backs, a reverse of the sickly girl on the back of the boy Father Al had seen on his first day in Korea. Father Al had his team of willing religious sisters, which by 1968 had grown to more than sixty in number. He wrote of the desperate need for what he called "mother-sisters":

> Of all the poor, helpless and destitute people in Korea, the poorest, the most helpless, and the most destitute is the orphan child. Not only does the orphan child lack the physical and material necessities in life, but what is more, he also lacks the spiritual and psychological requisites of a full life; namely, a mother's love and the warmth of a family.... [A Sister's] vocation is to give a mother's love and attention to the emotionally starved children entrusted to her. In doing so, the warmth and joy of true family life will be generated, and the orphan will have a chance to develop into normal people rather than soul-scarred alumni of institutions.[3]

As Father Al's orphan communities grew in size, an increasing number of young women from poor towns throughout Korea reached out to Father Al to express their desire to give their lives over to service to the poor. When the small orphanages and cottages finally reached their limit, he sought out a large area of unwanted land near his rectory, on Cheonma Mountain. Like with his first dispensary, the eight acres of barren earth was considered mostly valueless and disregarded real estate—but Father Al regarded it as a fitting spot to build his religious community's new motherhouse.

Even still, the new construction, which came at an especially high cost, posed an enormous dilemma for Father Al. Funding wasn't the issue; rather it was his long-held belief that contemporary housing and newness wrought havoc on vocations. He knew that the nuns' new home, which would overlook the open sea and be surrounded by twenty-three independent cottages for orphans, had to be austere and plain. He requested that architects design a serviceable two-story

[3] *StSi*, 145, 148.

building with small bedrooms and a chapel on the second-floor. Other than crucifixes on some walls, it would be entirely undecorated. He knew that the majority of new Catholic schools, convents, rectories, and churches in Korea and elsewhere routinely requested modern architectural flourishes and minor extravagances, but he condemned such add-ons, regarding them as dangerous drowning waves, obstacles to full identification with Christ and the poor and an embrace of the Cross. The memory of Sister Melfrieda's home-styled convent, and the Maryknolls' unruffled living standard, was marked indelibly in his conscience, especially during his days in his mountainside "poorhouse". Often scandalized by the poshness he had seen in chanceries, rectories, and convents of both clergy and nuns, Father Al concluded that holy religious lives demanded banishment of all comforts, profligate spending, and vanity.

When the motherhouse was completed on May 5, 1967, it could have been mistaken for a small country jail. No paved roads were within a mile. Because the chapel had no pews or chairs, the Sisters simply knelt on the floor during prayer. The new statue of the Virgin of the Poor that stood high up on the mountain behind the convent was surrounded not by rosebushes and decorative landscaping, but by wildflowers and clumps of tall ryegrass. Sisters often visited the site, where they knelt on a flat section of the mountainside to pray. He described the starkness and utility of the Sisters' new home in his writings:

> [The motherhouse], although strong and adequate, is quite simple and completely devoid of bell towers, verandas, and other architectural gingerbread.... The convent serves as a sign and a witness to poverty and humility not only to outsiders but, more important, to candidates entering the community as well. To a great extent, one's surroundings condition one's thinking. As Frank Lloyd Wright once put it: "First you form the building, then the building forms you." In the same line of reasoning, it is difficult to think poor while one is living rich and while one is psychologically identified with a convent which appears prestigious and imposing. The fact that the Mariahwe candidates live in a building of utmost simplicity facilitates a deeper penetration of the Christian ideal of poverty and service.[4]

[4] *Pov*, 76.

Father Al hoped that the sobriety of the motherhouse would lead the Sisters more deeply into an intimacy with Christ, a communion with the disregarded, a hunger for prayer, and a love of the Eucharist. The chapel's tabernacle was the convent's only ornate accoutrement, and at the end of long days the community spent time before it in candlelight, kneeling and quietly moving their lips in sacred silence before sleep. Without God's sanctifying graces, this religious community would never fully live out the cheerful self-denial of unyielding work.

"In a sense, our Sisters—the Sisters of Mary—could just as easily be called the 'Sisters of the Blessed Sacrament,'" Father Al wrote. "This little piece of bread is the secret of the Sisters of Mary and their apostolate. If one were to remove the Blessed Sacrament from one of our chapels, our work would quickly lose its vitality, wither up, and die."[5]

This first venture into major construction set the standard for the next thirty years, where he honored the same pared-down architectural approach. Each of the buildings he had erected in various parts of the world, many of which stretched seven stories high, would be as powerfully constructed and as vanilla in appearance. On the heels of the motherhouse came a large new middle school at the site of an old trash dump, which provided parents in the Amadong slums with free education for their children. Thereafter, the number of construction projects grew exponentially. When Father Al saw a pressing need, he would consult with the Sisters, call his small Korean Relief office about availability of funds, find some unwanted land, and dial the phone of a contractor.

Father Al knew he had to dedicate more of his time to helping the Sisters and visiting the beneficiaries of Korean Relief. He rose early each day to begin traveling from outreach to outreach, but as his missionary outposts for the poor expanded, he began to see that he lacked hours in the day to get to each site. In 1967, with Bishop Choi's consent, he handed over his Song-do parish pastorship to his associate pastor, in order to commit fully to his apostolate. Although he was the steward of enormous sums of money, he never kept a dollar on him; very often the only thing in his pocket was a rosary. If he saw the need for money in his travels, he contacted the motherhouse. Yet as he walked penniless from place to place, he saw the

[5] *TL*, 10, 12.

incomprehensible harvest that America's generosity and the work of his Korean religious community had brought to bear.

More than 800,000 Americans were donating consistently to Korean Relief by 1969. In the face of all the success, Father Al felt himself to be little and unworthy. He told the Sisters that their service should go completely unnoticed, except by the poor themselves. He believed God's finger of beneficence might point elsewhere if their work became publicized:

> Our God is a God of silence. He dwells in silence. When Jesus seeks the Father, He goes into the desert.... If we wish to serve really as children of God, we have to have a certain love of silence, a certain love of hiddenness, and a desire to serve without recognition, without noise, and without blowing your trumpet.... Many works of service of charity have failed. As I mentioned before, frequently, this serious lack is the fear of the cross, and fleeing from the cross. People want to serve without any suffering, pain, difficulty, or discomfort. This is not Christlike service. This type of service is not of value.... In order to serve the poor in a Christlike manner, in the name of Christ, we have to courageously renounce the praise, glory, recognition, and thanks of men. This requires courage. This requires sacrifice. This goes against our human nature....
>
> Our role, in a sense, is to cast the devil out of the children entrusted to us, the sick and the poor, and to fill them with the grace and life of God. This is to be done only by prayer accompanied by tears— [the tears of] prayer and sacrifice. The two go together—prayer and sacrifice—as flesh and blood. If you have flesh but no blood, you are pale, anemic, lifeless, weak and without vitality. Prayer without sacrifice is like flesh without blood. It is weak, anemic—ineffective....
>
> We come to serve the poor with the mind, the heart, the spirit of Christ—to serve the poor as He served the poor. We just realize that Christ served the poor especially spiritually. This was his focus, his thrust. His thirst was the soul rather than the body. It was eternity rather than time. It was the next world rather than this world.... He says, "I have come that my lambs might have life and that they might have it in abundance." These lambs, these sheep of Jesus are especially the poor, the lowly, the weak, the suffering. He comes to give them abundant life.[6]

[6] *Serm*, 2:21-23, 102, 230.

Faithful to Christ's day-to-day manner—and contrary to the Pharisees and rabbis who spent much of their days within synagogues during Christ's public ministry—Father Al and the Sisters walked from alley to alley and village to village to spend time entering the homes and places of the poor. Many, he knew, were ignorant of the Catholic faith. The priest was often seen teaching catechism to classrooms of orphans, leading Rosaries, hearing confessions, running or playing basketball and soccer with children, and giving spiritual talks to his religious community. He often stopped by to cheer on and tell jokes to the three-thousand-strong embroidery team. He regularly visited hospitals where he knelt at bedsides and prayed with tubercular patients. He crouched on the ground and spoke to sunken-cheeked beggars. He entered colonies for lepers, and reached for them.

One startling photograph exemplifies this dimension of his care in places permeated with death. Father Al is seen in the photo calmly washing the upper leg of a naked man in one of his beggar's homes. The man is clearly in agony; where his stomach should be, there is a black hole. Two other naked men sit nearby, sullen and severely hunched over; both appear to be leprous or infected with a skin disease. The accompanying caption mentions that Father Al contracted a "skin disease" that day. The Sisters of Mary with him in those early days say his care for the stomach-less man typified his work, where daily they watched their spiritual father kneel to clean, embrace, or pray with the poor and dying. It was this type of indelicate and often revolting form of provision he prioritized for his community:

Christ became as Lazarus. He not only left the banquet table and He not only left His Father's house, but He became Lazarus, He became the leper, the one who was hungry, despised, sick, suffering, and dying. In this way, He helped Lazarus. He restored him to health and gave him life and riches. This is Christ's approach to the service of the poor. It is very astounding. It is dramatic. This is the overwhelming Love of Christ....

[Saint Damien of Molokai] was the first who came and lived with [the lepers]. He shared their life and eventually he shared their disease. He became a leper himself. He took their suffering into his own body and his own flesh. It is a very difficult apostolate. One thing that repelled him was the stench.... Sometimes, in a confessional, he would go out and vomit, and come back and continue hearing confessions. Fr. Damien is very controversial because his character is very tough. He used to fight people and get in trouble with his bishop, but many of the saints were like this. But he was very heroic also....

What type of pain, or suffering, or sacrifice should we look for in our service to the poor? Basically, it is simply accepting with joy the inherent pain in the life of service, the suffering, and discomfort that God sends us each day. Each day, if we really serve the poor, we experience fatigue—we get tired—and discomfort with all these little children. You are in a room with fifty children and it is so hot, and it stinks, and really it is unpleasant. We lack rest, leisure, and free time. We are devoured by the poor. They eat us up like mosquitoes. We see this with Christ in the Gospel.[7]

Sister Michaela Kim, a pioneering Sister in the Mariahwe, continually paid witness to Father Al's one-to-one encounters with the poor. As one of the original twelve Sisters in the community, Sister Michaela became, in a sense, Father Al's right-hand woman in those early, frenetic days of Korean Relief. (Later, Father Al would appoint her as his successor in the order, giving her authority over all finances, personnel, expansion, and construction.) She saw him take on initiatives that had enormous costs in terms of money, planning, ingenuity, and management because, Sister Michaela felt, the Holy Spirit steered him to do things no one else would, to go places no one else would go. In 2003, more than four decades after her initial years of service, Sister Michaela recalled those booming early days of outreach:

[Father Al] said, "Love comes from God," so he continuously begged the Lord in prayer and in the Mass to fill him with love so as to be able to give that love to others. He tried to fulfill at all times the will of God even if it was difficult, even if he was criticized.

After long prayers, if he felt that was the will of God, he was ready to do it at all costs. For example: the beginning of the two congregations [the Sisters of Mary and the Brothers of Christ] and the expansion of his charity programs—many people warned him not to do it, but he took the risk in order to fulfill God's will, trusting in God's providence and grace. In spite of all the contradictions he pursued his plan in order to please Jesus and Mary.

[7] *Serm*, 2:8, 14, 16.

The primary motive why he was giving all the best services to the poor was to save their souls; [thus he] gave the humanitarian help through hospitals, schools, Boystowns, Girlstowns, home for unwed mothers, shelter for the beggars, and so on. He was doing all these things to save souls and give glory to God.[8]

As dozens of willing Sisters walked down the mountainside and filtered healing and hopeful light into the streets of Busan each morning, a very real renaissance of grace flowered in Bishop John Choi's Busan diocese. The bishop, Father Al's old traveling companion in America, watched much of it unfold. He occasionally shoveled the dirt at groundbreaking ceremonies and then months later cut the ribbon at openings for new orphanages, dispensaries, and the like. The bishop stood for photographs with small orphans in his arms; he shook politicians' hands as Father Al stood humbly by. Far in the background of many of the photographs, Sisters of Mary were often seen smiling or holding a child's hand.

As his orphanages and communities for the poor expanded, Father Al realized they were, little by little, by the grace of God and the hard work of the Sisters of Mary, taking on order and harmony. But something else was happening; large portions of the Korean city on the southern peninsula were undergoing transformation. Some slum communities were disappearing. Government officials, building contractors, the media, clergy of every denomination, and countless ordinary Koreans saw a substantial re-engineering of Busan's infrastructure—and most knew that the priest and Sisters who walked the streets each day were directly tied to it. They knew it was all being done in the name of the poor. It was a time of great grace in Busan, as the war-ravaged city began slowly to ease away from the aftershocks of war. At the same time, the growing Catholic Church in Korea was undergoing a rebirth.

Father Al knew, though, that wolves were circling.

[8] Pos, 137-38.

10

Storms

Tensions with the Bishop, 1965–1970

NO MATTER HOW OVERWHELMED his life became by the volume of his work, Father Al broke away each day to run. Before a lunch of a stirred glass of orange Tang and a small peanut butter sandwich, he disappeared into the hills and alleyways of Busan. Early on, his escapes served as revelatory gallops through fields of poverty, where he was able to set his eyes on the city's loneliest and most neglected people. These places would soon be visited by him and the willing helpers from the Sisters of Mary.

As time moved on in Busan, Father Al acquired the legs and lungs of a marathoner. He laced his sneakers and ran every day regardless of bitter cold, noonday heat, or even the lingering effects of a passing monsoon. In the process of getting to know every corner of the city, Father Al at the end of the 1960s was in the best physical shape of his life. He turned his runs into tests of endurance that often lasted up to an hour; the workouts allowed him to discard mental burdens and create an interior silence. Even during more intense workouts, when his legs churned like a racehorse's in the frenzy of a stretch run, he prayed, with his mind like a quiet chapel.

Saint Paul's letters spoke powerfully to Father Al, and he took seriously the apostle's words in 1 Corinthians to run so as to win the race (9:24). He wanted to bring discipline and mortification even to his leisure. His brother Lou said that in exercise—when his lungs burned, his perennially sore hip flared, and his breathing became labored—Father Al daily stretched the limits of his body in order to draw closer to Christ.

"He always had his beat-up running shoes", Lou recounted. "His feet hurt, his legs hurt and after a while, his whole body would hurt. I think it's because he wanted to unite himself fully with Christ. He was so rigorous with himself on his runs because he knew if he was going to attempt to bring Jesus to every corner of the earth, he had to have resolve. He didn't want to waste his time running if he wasn't able to enter into prayer and union with Christ. Maybe a way of putting it is that he was *collecting* the Spirit on those runs."

In *Killing Me Softly*, the autobiography that Father Al dictated before his death, he revealed that his runs also served a practical purpose. "It was a marvelous release.... The increase of oxygen to the brain stimulated the creative process and helped greatly to resolve problems and solve difficulties that were troubling me."[1]

As Father Al ran Busan's hills in 1969, it was mostly Bishop Choi who was on his mind. This humble friend, who had simply cut off his boot heels when told they were meant for a woman, had begun to sabotage his priesthood. The same man with whom he had shared weeks of cramped car space during their American begging tour had begun to calumniate him. If he had been given the power, Bishop Choi would have exiled the American priest from his land. "I was there when all of this began to unfold", Monsignor Golasinski disclosed. "Bishop Choi tried everything to go after him—but Father Al knew Christ was on his side. He had this total confidence in him."

THE FISSURE STARTED BENIGNLY ENOUGH, in 1965, when Bishop Choi asked Father Al to begin reshaping the discipline of the Sisters of Mary order, which had already attained its identity throughout his diocese as an order that directly served the poorest of the poor. The bishop wanted the Sisters to receive more education and eventually work as teachers in Busan's small number of overcrowded Catholic schools. Father Al was jarred by this request. Just a year before, the bishop had warmly embraced the Sisters of Mary's charism. Father Al worried that an intellectual apostolate would ring the death knell for their original mission—direct, humble care for the poor—and prove crushing to many thousands of Busan's most destitute. The proposal reminded him of his time with the Maryknolls, when formators had

[1] *KMS*, 20.

nudged him away from a life in the mission fields and into one behind the desk or podium. Something was wrong here, and he believed that Church teaching agreed.

Five years after the formation of the Sisters of Mary, Father Al spent a great deal of time studying the Second Vatican Council's document entitled *Perfectae caritatis*, a decree on the renewal of religious life. He believed it was indispensable, revealing Christ as one who cried out through the voices of the poor. The Church was in desperate need of witnesses willing to endure torment and persecution in proclaiming the gospel throughout the globe. *Perfectae caritatis* begged for missionaries to serve as did the first disciples, who traveled with little more than a tunic, a staff, and a zeal to spread the good news of God's love. To Father Al, the document spelled out in clear terms that missionary communities and religious orders should launch out into foreign lands to preach as John the Baptist and serve as Saint Vincent de Paul—both of whom threw off every comfort. *Perfectae caritatis* gave missionaries a mandate to offer themselves as a holocaust to spread the one, true Catholic faith:

> Since the Church has accepted their surrender of self they should realize they are also dedicated to its service. This service of God ought to inspire and foster in them the exercise of the virtues, especially humility, obedience, fortitude and chastity. In such a way they share in Christ's emptying of Himself (cf. Phil. 2:7) and His life in the spirit (cf. Rom. 8:1–13). Faithful to their profession then, and leaving all things for the sake of Christ (cf. Mark 10:28), religious are to follow Him (cf. Matt. 19:21) as the one thing necessary (cf. Luke 10:42) listening to His words (cf. Luke 10:39) and solicitous for the things that are His (cf. 1 Cor. 7:32). It is necessary therefore that the members of every community, seeking God solely and before everything else, should join contemplation, by which they fix their minds and hearts on Him, with apostolic love, by which they strive to be associated with the work of redemption and to spread the kingdom of God.[2]

In Father Al's view, by asking him to remold the Sisters' charism, Bishop Choi was unwittingly requesting that he betray Mary's call to

---

[2] Vatican Council II, Decree on the Adaptation and Renewal of Religious Life *Perfectae caritatis* (October 28, 1965).

him in Banneux. Our Lady's words to Mariette—"I come to relieve the sick. . . . I come to relieve suffering"—were *his*, the torch she had passed on to him, which he now was sharing with the Sisters of Mary. Her call was inviolable and holy. The Sisters' crucified path of temporal and spiritual aid for those living in poverty, out of a contemplative love for Christ, was indeed *the better part*. Advanced degrees, human wisdom, and classroom instruction could be attained by someone else.

Father Al told his bishop no.

He reminded Bishop Choi of what unfolded every day in his diocese: the Sisters of Mary brought constant care to every ghetto and mountainside hovel, beneath every bridge, and into each of the city's abysmally run social welfare centers. They were never off the clock in Busan's dark archipelagos of prisons, orphanages, mental wards, dispensaries, old age homes, leper colonies, and homes for widows and unmarried mothers. Through the sweat of their brow and through cheerful self-denial, the Sisters *themselves* were becoming the revamped welfare system of the Korean port town.

Father Al could not, in good conscience, deviate from the order's foundational mission. Willing and able teachers could be found anywhere, he told him, and many of the Second Vatican Council's documents underscored the importance of orders remaining faithful to their original charism. Bishop Choi, who considered the priest's vow of obedience of far greater import, walked away from the discussion frustrated—and a cold war was born. Their relationship would never be the same.

FATHER AL FILLED HIS SIXTEEN-TO-EIGHTEEN-HOUR WORKDAYS by broadening the reach of his services to the poor and obliging the spiritual duties of his priesthood, which included the celebration of daily Mass and hearing many dozens of confessions each day. He gave frequent Bible meditations, theology classes, spiritual conferences, and retreats to the Sisters. So busy was Father Al that he had mostly forgotten about the odd request from his bishop. Like a proud and doting father, he watched the "mother-sisters" develop into the southern city's most valued population of temporal and spiritual helpers. They bathed and clothed naked itinerants, slaved over severely developmentally disabled children and teens, and gathered unwanted orphans into their arms each day. They knew lepers by their first names. Because of their work, many hundreds who should have died—lived.

Sister Catherine Kim, who was in Busan in those early days, shared a searing memory of the type of work she took on each day:

> My first job was to take care of ten eight-to-twelve-year-old severely disabled kids. They were not able to appropriately communicate and had very limited mobility. Father Al used to call them "the most precious Jesus". He made routine visits to make sure that the kids were well taken care of.
>
> Most of the kids in that class didn't know what to do with their own feces and urine. Sometimes they would play with their feces and throw it on the wall. There were kids who ate until vomiting and then swallowed their vomit. Kids drank chemicals and pulled food out of other kids' mouths. Kids screamed continuously and spat on other kids' faces. Some kids talked to themselves all day. I always tried to remind myself that the precious Jesus was living in the pain inside of these children. So in those days, I devoted myself to them.
>
> The daily assignment started at 4 A.M. When I entered the kids' room, it was heavy with the toxic smell of their urine and excrement. They had left marks all over the walls and floor. I remember once when one of the children brought his excrement to me on his dinner plate. He had no idea what he did. He just smiled at me with pride. . . . The first thing I did for the kids was to give them a bath, one by one, and change them into fresh clothes. I hand-washed dirty clothes and sanitized the room to make it clean and safe. In winter, I was drenched with sweat even though it was cold. . . .
>
> Except for Mass and hourly liturgy times, my eyes were fixed to the kids all day long: feeding, cleaning rooms, brushing their teeth, changing diapers, and washing them all day long. To maintain their health, I walked the grounds with them. We were like a family. By that time, I was able to communicate with them eye-to-eye, heart-to-heart.

As time moved on, Father Al saw indications that Bishop Choi had never left the dispute behind; in fact, it seemed to have embittered him. In 1966, the bishop refused Father Al's invitation to provide the blessing for the opening of newly built Mariahwe orphanages behind his Song-do parish. On a June afternoon a year later, Bishop Choi joined with several Korean bishops and dozens of priests for the reopening of Father Al's new "Beggars' Hospital" in the Amadong slum, delivering an indirect twenty-minute attack on the work of Korean Relief and the Sisters of Mary. Although Father Al was unsurprised by his comments, he noticed a few Sisters at the groundbreaking who were stunned and "brokenhearted". Thereafter, Bishop Choi was mostly absent from Masses and events Father Al attended. Clergy shared with the American priest that his bishop became visibly upset when his name came up in conversation. He spoke poorly of him.

In November 1969, Father Al discovered that two members of his religious community had endured an "angry attack" by Bishop Choi when he visited the motherhouse. "When he [confronted] the Sisters, Bishop Choi had poked the hornet's nest", opined Monsignor Golasinski, who would be an eyewitness to the unraveling relationship between Father Al and his bishop. "And when you poke a man as bold as Aloysius Schwartz, things are not going to become easy for you."

On December 3, 1969, Schwartz composed a long, at times barbed letter in defense of the Sisters' work. The following is an excerpt:

Your Excellency,

The following Memorandum is prompted by your recent visit to the Mariahwe on Monday, Nov. 17. At this time—during my absence—you summoned the two Sisters in charge and stated angrily that the Mariahwe program of formation was wrong and should be completely changed. By way of reply, I submit the following facts for your reflection. . . .

Does the training program of the Mariahwe in any way run counter to existing Church Law or Church Directives? I have posed this question to Canon Lawyers and they have assured me and reassured me that in no way do we violate the law of the Church governing the formation and training of religious . . . . I am convinced that the training program now in force at the Mariahwe adheres completely not only to the spirit of those decrees but even to their letter. . . .

This "following of Christ" who had no formal education, no diplomas, and no degrees is basic, fundamental, and essential; everything else is secondary and unimportant. . . . The Mariahwe Sisters were founded in answer to the needs—not of other countries—but of the very poor in Korea.

The training of the Mariahwe Sisters is in view of the purpose for which they were founded, namely to serve the very poor and destitute in simplicity and humility. If middle, high school, and college diplomas were necessary to achieve this end we would not hesitate to obtain them. Such diplomas would tend to turn the Sisters aside from their original vocation of direct service to the poorest. It would create a psychological and emotional gap between themselves and the very poor who usually do not even have primary school education. With diplomas, our Sisters would find direct service a waste of their education and eventually move into administrative roles only. Eventually, they would move away from the poor altogether and end up by administering to the needs of those who are more intellectually attractive such as students and the rich.

Apparently, you must be convinced that our Sisters are doing a very poor job to be so displeased with them and to insist on changing our method of formation. The objective fact is, however, the Mariahwe Sisters are serving the poor in a most effective manner .... In 3 months time the Mariahwe Sisters have taken over the Busan Beggars' Hospital and have completely transformed it. They constantly visit the poor in the slums, they teach catechism to them. They visit mental institutes. They have two old age homes. And so on. Is there any other group of religious sisters in Korea—with or without formal education and diplomas—who are doing effective work for the poor? ...

During the 5 years which have elapsed since the Mariahwe began, we have had many difficulties, problems, and headaches. It has been a real struggle for us, but during this time never once—not once—have we received a single word of fatherly encouragement or praise from you. On the contrary, we have repeatedly been the object of your ill temper and displeasure....

As bishop—as pastor, as father, as apostle—should you not give full support and encouragement to [the Sisters] whose only desire in life is not proud diplomas or worldly degrees but to serve the poorest of Korea in silence, humility, and poverty? I would be most grateful for a written reply to these reflections.... You may wonder why I express so boldly my thoughts to you. The reason is you have repeatedly invited your priests to express directly and clearly to you their complaints—rather than to go behind your back.[3]

In the weeks following Bishop Choi's broadside against the Sisters, Father Al also began to look more closely at his bishop's disbursements of Korean Relief donations. What he discovered was disturbing: Bishop Choi had been misallocating funds for years. "Fr. Al noticed

[3] *Pos*, 379–81.

that most of [his] projects were phony", recalled Damiano. "Their schools and hospitals were money-making projects, not for the poor people."[4]

When Father Al formed Korean Relief in Washington D.C. in 1961, he gradually began to allot Bishop Choi a share of the donations to use at his discretion. They agreed all disbursements of the donations would go to serve the poor in the strictest sense; Father Al had written as much into Korean Relief's founding documents. Because he had always considered his bishop aligned with his mission, he never felt the need to review his apportionments.

Yet Bishop Choi's accounting records, reviewed by Father Al in 1969, showed he had been using donations for construction enterprises and land purchases and to pay down diocesan debt. He donated to unnamed state-run projects. Between 1963 and 1968, he had allotted more than $400,000 to various church programs. During the same span, he distributed more than $5,000 to his relatives and members of the clergy. A small sampling of Bishop Choi's accounting ledger from 1965 to 1966 is reflective of what Father Al believed to be an abuse of discretionary funds:

> May 1965—Land Procurement—Tong Rae Church—$2,600.00
> May 1965—Fr. Hang, Yeng Chun—$500.00
> May 1965—Land Procurement—Jendo Dong and Yenji Dong—$3,000
> July 1965—Agricultural Center—$1,350.00
> August 1965—Governor's Relief Project—$1,355.00
> August 1965—Bishop Ji—$1,350.00
> August 1966—Preparation for Bishop Chang's Consecration—$578.00
> August 1966—Sonmok Minor Seminary, Taegu—$2,000.00
> September 1966—Farming Project, Chejudo—$3,500.00
> September 1966—River Bank Construction—$3,000.00
> November 1966—Land in front of Busan Railway Station—$11,410.00[5]

When his allocation of the donations became clear in 1969, Father Al cut off all Korean Relief distributions to Bishop Choi, who was

[4] *Pos*, 591.
[5] PM.

powerless to prevent it. He removed the bishop's name from all mailers and told him his involvement with Korean Relief was over. He considered the bishop's allotments irreconcilable and even indictable in a court of law. Yet the fact that Bishop Choi kept such clear records is revelatory; he believed his distributions to be above-board and of merit. When Father Al first confronted him about his desertion from the mission, his bishop claimed his stewardship was inspired, explaining, for example, that his land purchases were meant for the locations of future church construction. He said his foresight would pave the way for a strong Catholic Church in Korea. In full disagreement, Father Al rebuked his decisions and countered that tens of thousands of Korean Relief donors were non-Catholics who had no interest in expanding Catholicism in South Korea; he said Americans gave donations to help to save the lives of the poor and war-ravaged, not to build churches in his diocese. The stalemate grew fractious. In the ensuing months, Bishop Choi demanded access to the distributions through a steady stream of pleas, letters, and justifications. Father Al remained inflexible; his bishop would never receive another nickel.

The removal of the purse strings turned what had simply been a relationship turned sour into a pugilistic chorus of calumnies and verbal attacks against Father Al and the Sisters of Mary, and innumerable threats to remove his faculties. Bishop Choi formed a nine-man committee of priests who attempted to convince Father Al to resume disbursements; the clergy pointed to the vow of obedience he had taken to Bishop Choi after being incardinated into his diocese. When that failed in the fall of 1969, Bishop Choi repeatedly threatened to shut down the Sisters of Mary and halt all ongoing building projects, including a large home for vagrant boys and the long-planned Mariahwe Mercy Hospital—but Father Al told the building contractors to keep on schedule. A popular magazine, the Korean equivalent to the American periodical *Life*, published a long piece insinuating a romantic link between Father Al and a religious sister in his community. In the piece, Bishop Choi didn't defend the American priest.

Throughout it all, Father Al seemed rather amused by his bishop's sustained throwing of sand into the gears. "The money was designated for the poor and I felt it was not being used for this sacred purpose", Father Al wrote. "My bishop let out a kind of primal scream that could be heard as far as North Korea. He literally struck the table and I felt that he was very close to striking me.... The fact that [his] desires were thwarted is a tribute to the grace and mercy of God."[6]

At his most desperate point, Bishop Choi wrote a letter to Pope Paul VI that disparaged Father Al. He requested the pope's help in controlling the renegade American missionary, who had "an attitude of mind" that was "extremely questionable". That tactic not only failed, but completely backfired. Three weeks after receiving his letter, on June 18, 1970, the pope dispatched to Busan a Maryknoll priest named Father Michael Zunno, who would serve as an apostolic visitor to investigate the circumstances behind the falling out. As chance would have it, the pope asked Father Zunno to send his findings to none other than Father Al's old friend, Cardinal Agagianian— the same prelate who had once blithely encouraged him in his work, even in the face of the American bishops' distress over lost donations.

Six weeks of more than ninety interviews helped Father Zunno to determine that "the nature and character of Bishop Choi is the problem.... It surprised me that even those who support Bishop Choi publicly, freely mentioned to me faults in his nature", he wrote in the comprehensive report sent to Cardinal Agagianian.[7] He suggested that Bishop Choi immediately be given a vicar general with active power to help administer the Church in Busan.

In short order, Bishop Gabriel Lee was made an auxiliary bishop— and Father Al went on unabated. "Father Al never flagged throughout the attacks, even when his bishop wouldn't help him out of the false hanky-panky allegation", Monsignor Golasinski said. "But Father Al was as good a counter puncher as there ever was. He was as combative at fighting things he knew were wrong as anyone I knew."

Monsignor Golasinski continued: "There was never a hint in him that showed he didn't think God was on his side. He stood on the side of the right and the just, and he knew it. He knew the Lord was with him.... He never had a doubt he would prevail. He just fought till the end."

AFTER FINALLY DISTANCING HIMSELF FROM HIS BISHOP, Father Al was able to turn his attention to what had been on his mind for more than

---

[6] KMS, 58.
[7] Pos, 448.

a year. He wanted to purchase the least desirable piece of real estate in Busan; he wanted ownership and control of the city-run Beggars' Hospice. It was a forlorn facility that served as a home for societal outcasts, drifters, and the tubercular. It offered a place off the streets, but little more. Father Al had absorbed its deplorable conditions while visiting with members of his religious community after Mass each Sunday. Together, they bathed, cut the hair, and clipped the nails of Busan's unwanted. They brought little gifts, read Scripture, prayed, and sang to each resident. In their own unassuming way, they tried to coax life back into dry bones. But because city employees had taken such poor care of them for so long, Father Al and the Sisters could do nothing to slow the alarming death rate. There were no funerals. Perched high on a hill, the Beggars' Hospice seemed one of the loneliest places on earth—which is why Father Al hungered for it. He knew the potential it had for Easter resurrection.

He purchased the hospice, explaining in his journals the reason for the takeover and its subsequent transformation:

> I read somewhere where one of the signs of diabolical possession was the overwhelming stench of human excrement emanating from the individual in question. If this is so, then the devil was very much present at the Beggars' Hospice. The place was also overrun by lice, bugs, insects, and in summer was infested with swarms of flies and mosquitoes. Adequate funds were allocated for food and medical treatment, but there was no supervision. The staff was poorly paid, the food was filthy, and the medicine was sold, money pocketed, and in general, the people were left to their own despair.
>
> The death rate was atrocious. At that time, out of 120 inmates, there were between twenty and thirty deaths a month. The bodies were disposed of as so much garbage. They were simply wrapped in a straw mat which was placed in a hand cart. One of the men working at the Beggars' Hospice pushed the cart four or five miles to a pauper's cemetery where the body was dumped in a shallow grave on the side of a mountain with a small wooden marker to indicate its presence. A number of bodies were sold to the University Hospital for medical purposes. A nice profit was realized in this fashion from those working at the Beggars' Hospice.
>
> I then contacted the Mayor and asked him to turn the Beggars' Hospice over to the Mariahwe Sisters. After considerable red tape and delay, a contract was signed and the Sisters officially took over the

place. Initially, we operated the Beggars' Hospice at our own expense. As soon as the city officials left us alone, we rolled up our sleeves and went to work. Patients were bathed, cleaned and washed, and given a change of fresh clothing. The task was not as simple as it may sound. Many of the people were filthy beyond description. Some had suspicious looking diseases. But the Sisters were a courageous lot and the work progressed nicely. I took away a souvenir from that first day at the Beggars' Hospice. I contracted a skin infection from bathing the inmates which left me with inflamed fingers for about six or eight months. Apparently the fury of Satan was aroused by our trespassing into this private hell and this was one way of getting back at me.

Little by little we got on top of things. I contacted a group of engineers at the United States Army base. They came out and fumigated the place. We painted the walls and the cement floor. We painted the outside of the building and erected a third building which contained a small chapel, dispensary, and quarters for the Sisters who were in charge of the Beggars' Hospice. I contacted a psychiatrist who advised us and counseled us on how to treat the mentally disturbed patients. And, after a few months, the death rate dropped drastically from twenty or thirty a month to two or three a month. What is more, the patients no longer had that concentration camp type of look. Although many were terminally ill, the patients themselves could not believe the transformation that was brought on in such a short period of time. They said it was like the difference between heaven and hell. The Hospice has been spiritualized. The patients were taught in a very gentle, quiet manner about God. They were encouraged to help each other. They were encouraged to pray, and many of them spent long hours in the chapel. This emphasis on the spiritual has proven itself very beneficial not only to the souls of the patients but to their bodies as well. It creates an atmosphere of hope and optimism which is so conducive to recovery.[8]

In the summer of 1969, Father Al had found himself the custodian of three dispensaries treating, on average, a total of 1,500 patients a day. He also began a tubercular clinic that treated up to 100 patients each day. He told his medical staff not to charge a dime for care; he would find the money to pay their salaries and for medicine. Hundreds of orphans were already in his charge, and now he was elbow

[8] PM.

deep in the work of turning around the Beggars' Hospice. Builders had just completed a large middle school he had financed for poor children in the slums.

Then Father Al came up against a man who wanted him dead. His name was Lee Soon Young. He was the most dangerous man on the Korean peninsula. "Father Al always called him 'Big Daddy'. But that put a nice spin on it", Monsignor Golasinski explained. "The man was a monster."

The Loneliest Superhero

Encounter with the Kingpin, 1966–1975

THERE WAS A TIME when all little Al Schwartz wanted was to be a hero who put down villains. The resolve of the four high-spirited comic book orphans—André, Alfie, Brooklyn, and Jan, the Boy Commandos—impacted him as powerfully as when his mother knelt down beside him at night to pray. In a remarkable way, throughout his nearly sixty-two years of life, Father Al found that his ambitions, deepest desires, and even starry-eyed boyhood dreams invariably had a way of always coming back to him, but in surprising forms.

One of the most dark-hearted men in South Korea, Lee Soon Young, seemed to come right off the pages of a *Boy Commandos* comic book. His rise in power surged virtually unchecked across Busan, whose police, legislators, and mayor mostly cowered before him. They knew he had dirt on seemingly the entire Far East, including them.

Soon Young had a full-moon face attached to a body built like a bulldozer. He swaggered slowly when he walked, like an overloaded Chevy pickup with a swerving tail. He had a kingpin's laugh, a high-pitched cackle that carried across rooms. Most of what he said was either a threat, a lie, a scheme, or a combination of each. He spoke in vulgarities and didn't much care if a religious sister overheard. Loathsome characters and hardened criminals feared him, and passersby kept their heads down when they got near him. He was certainly a goon, but he wasn't dumb; he graduated from Chosun University with a degree in liberal arts and eventually rose to the rank of lieutenant in the South Korean Army. But when he found he was unable to get his hands on as much money as he desired, vice entered him.

After seven years of military service, Soon Young moved into social welfare management work. After discovering multiple ways to game the system, he launched into what can only be viewed as a gruesome steamrolling of humanity, a coarse betrayal of the centuries-strong Korean code of decency and honor. Soon Young deceived, stole, extorted, tortured, and, many believed, murdered to expand his enterprise. Monsignor Golasinski claims the man exported pigs to Japan with bellies full of narcotics. He sold to local bakers the Australian wheat earmarked for the residents under his care. He sold clothes meant for orphans on the streets and to thrift stores, knowing that the children in his compound would be too ashamed to attempt an escape. At its height, this community for the homeless, which lay only a few hundred yards away from Father Al's Beggars' Hospice, had 1,200 residents. He used every one of them to acquire more wealth. "In all truth, he was a genius at corruption", Monsignor Golasinski judged. "And he had the entire west side of Busan in his pocket. We knew he had an older brother in the General Assembly who was working with him."

Already at the outset of his social-service career he began building his empire. After purchasing a state-subsidized home for abandoned lepers, he convinced the societal outcasts in his charge to become the foundation of his fledgling criminal syndicate. Although the majority of lepers were dormant, Soon Young knew just the thought of them instilled fear in the world outside; he knew their rank odor, bodily disfigurements, and haggardness could frighten future adversaries into submission. Within a year, his gang of lepers had become renowned in Busan, having spread out everywhere to do their boss' bidding. It wasn't uncommon to see a leper rubbing his diseased limb across the body of one of Soon Young's horrified foes. This made up just a small fraction of his operation.

Soon Young began to grow his crime network on the back of a questionable governmental policy that sought to "clean the streets" of a rising tide of homeless people brought on by the war. Soon Young volunteered to be a "cleaner". A contract was drawn up for him to relocate homeless itinerants to his compound in the hills, Jae-saengwon. One clause was of particular interest to Soon Young: he would be paid for every warm body he brought in. The more home-less and developmentally challenged street people he "collected", the more money he was awarded. If someone in his custody died, this was no problem for Soon Young. He would merely dispatch his gang of lepers and ex-convicts to the streets at night to find replacements. Because Soon Young was pocketing government subsidies and selling the majority of relief goods and medicine on the black market, the malnourished residents at Jaesaengwon, many of whom were children orphaned by the war, often withered away and died. Their bodies were disposed of at night on a mountain behind the complex. Moonlight guided the shovels.

"It became known that he would bury a body, then plant a pine tree to camouflage and mark the death", Monsignor Golasinski said. "All of his residents were malnourished, diseased, and beaten. If any rose up to buck the system, they would just disappear." He went on: "People were beaten all the time. Ambulance drivers were always pulling up to the place.... The place was run by ex-cons, draft dodgers, and gangs. Really, the place was a death house. Over seven hundred bodies were buried on that hill."

SCHWARTZ HAD ALREADY GOTTEN A CLOSE-UP LOOK AT CRIME in his first parish. Days after becoming pastor at Song-do Church, he discovered that a long-time catechist was spearheading a criminal ring. For years he had been stealing and selling parish charitable goods on the Korean black market. Only a portion of the goods brought in by Catholic Relief Services—flour, cornmeal, beans, and medicine— was making its way to its intended poor parishioners. One of Father Al's first acts as pastor was firing the catechist. Damiano, who helped expose the corruption, dealt with the fallout, which he detailed in his self-published book *Father Al Schwartz, Who Is Still Alive*.

> One night, angered by the sudden change and the stoppage of their income, the catechist's son came to me and requested to meet him in an empty house located in front of the church building. He said that he had something to discuss with me. I thought that I had no reason to refuse his demand because I didn't want to look like a coward.
>
> In that empty house, I found he wasn't alone. He was with his friend gangsters. At first, they tried to win my favors with tender words. Then they suggested that we become friends and sell some relief goods of which distribution was under my control. As the dialogue didn't go as they expected, they started to threaten me. They

said they could even kill me. They didn't realize that I had just left the army and for whom I was working. When they found their [threats] didn't work, they finally let me go.

After his experience at Song-do, Father Al saw that widespread corruption, bribes, and the reselling of stolen relief goods permeated large swaths of Korean government institutions, social welfare systems, and Catholic parishes. But he had not yet seen anything like Soon Young's operation.

One day, Father Al looked across the street from the Beggars' Hospice and noticed for the first time some low-lying nondescript cement buildings near a bit of reclaimed swampland. Much of the complex was concealed by gray cinder-block walls and overgrown weeds. The buildings lay sixty or so yards off the main road. Father Al thought it was a complex of army barracks left over from the war, or perhaps an old chicken-slaughtering factory. "The place had a strange aura about it", Damiano Park quotes him as saying.[1] After some time, one of the Sisters told him she occasionally heard strange sounds, like flesh being beaten with clubs, coming from the complex across the road. Later, a few other Sisters said they thought they had heard barely audible wails or rhythmic groans at night, from what sounded like children. This was Jaesaengwon.

Father Al had no idea of the magnitude of the evil operation unfolding across the street from the Beggars' Hospice until one afternoon a small girl zombied into the building. Her appearance appalled them; she was skeletal, bruised, hollow-eyed, and apparently tubercular. She spoke sparingly, but a small medical staff and some Sisters learned she had been at Soon Young's compound for more than a year. A few days later, like a small candle being blown out, the girl died.

The death of the poor girl incensed Father Al. He had already been rattled earlier that month when an elderly man who had escaped from Jaesaengwon staggered into the hospice with a severe head wound. He, too, died shortly thereafter. Father Al shared his emotions after the girl's death in his personal writings:

I will never forget the pathetic look of resignation in her eyes. No attempt had been made to treat her or help her in any way.... This

[1] Damiano Park, *Father Al Schwartz, Who Is Still Alive* (self-pub.), 26–27.

little girl helped me make up my mind. I felt I should do something to help these people. They were my neighbors, they were right next door to me, and as such they reminded me of Lazarus at the rich man's door. However, these people, unlike Lazarus, did not even have a dog to lick their sores and relieve their pain. They were utterly abandoned.[2]

Father Al knew it was time to act. "St. Ambrose has said: 'If you meet a beggar dying of hunger in the street, and you refuse him food, you in effect have killed him'", he reflected. "We had similar moral feelings towards the children detained at Jaesaengwon. We were in a position to help them. If we refused, turned our backs, and walked away from them, we in effect would be killing them, and in a sense, be guilty of murder."

He crossed the street and covertly investigated. It was a place where street children, beggars, vagrants, and the mentally insane were tortured and left for dead on a routine basis. Father Al described the discovery in his journals:

The place was a modern-day Korean version of a concentration camp. Just as during World War II the Nazis rounded up undesirable citizens and concentrated them into certain defined areas, so these poor people were rounded up from the streets, alleys, railway stations, and under the bridges of Busan and concentrated at this place. It was called the *Jaesaengwon*, a Korean term which roughly translated means "new life." However, the people interned there looked more like death warmed over.[3]

A gang of ex-convicts patrolled the complex, which had been entrusted to Soon Young by the city. Father Al painted the sickening conditions in detail:

At any given time there were usually about 1,200 inmates at the camp, men, women, and children, of all ages and all types. There were a number of criminal elements among these people, a number of mentally deranged people, and also a certain number of people who were

[2] PM.
[3] PM.

handicapped or crippled. Many of the inmates, especially the children, showed signs of malnutrition, eye infection, skin disease, and in some cases, incipient tuberculosis....

I learned that many of the kids periodically tried to escape. The camp was ringed by guards at night, and it required enormous courage on the part of the kids to attempt a breakout. If they got caught, the kids were severely beaten or tortured. Lit cigarettes were applied to the soles of their feet. Or else the soles of their feet were beaten with a heavy wooden stick. A number of the kids ended up with deformed limbs as a result of such abuse. As can be imagined, there were not only a number of serious injuries but deaths as well among the inmates.... I later learned that many of the women and girls were molested by the guards and by those in charge.[4]

Father Al began compiling an extensive report of what he gathered about Soon Young's criminal activity. He soon had photographic evidence and firsthand testimony from former residents of inhuman forms of physical and psychological abuse. Local officials and police, though—each of whom knew Soon Young on a first-name basis— told him they wouldn't investigate his claims. Devastated by their inaction and fear in the face of the diabolical, Father Al sent his report to state officials in Seoul. President Park Chung-hee, his attorney general, and the minister of health and social welfare each received a copy. Days later, investigators found enough evidence of wrongdoing to arrest Soon Young. "The local press jumped on the story with glee. They described Big Daddy as a vampire who sucked the blood of innocent children", Father Al wrote in his journal. "They were very eloquent and self-righteous as long as Big Daddy was safely behind bars."[5]

His jail time lasted less than two weeks; Soon Young was released on a technicality. Remarkably, Father Al discovered soon thereafter that Bishop Choi helped in securing his release. Father Al suspected what his bishop, perhaps, was hoping. "Big Daddy came roaring out of the cooler breathing fire and brimstone", Father Al recounted in his journal. "After [he] got out of prison, he came after me."[6]

[4] PM.
[5] PM.
[6] PM.

With little to no help from state authorities, Father Al sought the aid of Church leaders and fellow clergy, many dozens of whom signed a petition substantiating Father Al's claims of Soon Young's rampant criminality and abuse of his residents. A short while later, though, all but twenty-three of the priests asked their names to be removed. Word of their signatures had gotten back to Soon Young, who threatened their lives.

Although Soon Young and his gang intensified their threats against Father Al and his religious community, they seem to have been little more than a minor annoyance. Schwartz told the Sisters he knew God would eventually take the nuisance off their hands. One of the imperatives from Our Lady of Banneux was the command to relieve the poor and suffering, and demolishing Big Daddy's empire was part of that command. In his eyes, the Sisters of Mary and Damiano were the humble band of little Commandos that Mary had given to him— and that was good enough. Against all odds, he believed Soon Young would be overcome, not by him, but by Our Lady of Banneux.

Father Al expressed in his journal:

> Big Daddy played by a completely different set of rules.... He had no scruples about resorting to threats and violence nor about using money to influence reporters, investigators, prosecutors, government officials. Nor did he have any qualms about using lies and deceits as they served his purpose.... However, one thing the Sisters and I had going for us was the firm conviction that what we were doing was right, sort of a moral imperative, if you will, from which great strength is derived.[7]

Father Al was mindful of what the apostle Paul wrote about individuals like Soon Young: "Their end is destruction, their god is their belly, and they glory in their shame" (Phil 3:19). He knew that the man would, in time, be destroyed by his own hand. Still, the awareness didn't make Father Al's situation any more comfortable. "I was watched twenty-four hours a day by some of his hoodlums", the priest wrote. "I found them at times on the roof of my house at night." Soon Young was also keeping an eye on escapees and turncoats.[8]

[7] PM.
[8] PM.

One night, one of Soon Young's guards "defected to us", Father Al said. The anxious man, visibly frightened by his decision to leave the compound, requested their protection for the night. After settling down, he began to unpack the cycle of mistreatment of Jaesaengwon's residents. Late that night, for reasons unknown, he left the safety of the Beggars' Hospice. He was found the next day in a stairwell with a fractured skull, dead. Police determined there had been "an accidental fall".

Later that year, a seventeen-year-old boy escaped Jaesaengwon and took up residence at the hospice. He shared detailed accounts—dates, times, circumstances—of five killings he had witnessed. He knew the identities of the murderers. Father Al submitted the teenager's sworn testimony to Busan's attorney general and chief of police. Within a week, the brave young man disappeared and was never seen again. His claims were never investigated. The teenager's unflinching courage served as an instrument for justice and a reminder that the fight he had picked with Soon Young could never be abandoned. The boy's sacrifice animated Father Al to step even further into his own sacrifice, to battle even harder. This was becoming warlike. He prayed, fasted, and asked for another way—and an idea came.

Aware Soon Young's reign would continue unabated without the help of Busan's magistrate, Father Al devised a plan reminiscent of the famed German industrialist Oskar Schindler, who helped to save the lives of 1,200 Jews by employing them in his factories. Father Al arranged for a meeting with Soon Young and offered him $750,000 for his Jaesaengwon complex. It was ransom money. The facility itself was a charnel house to be burned to the ground; Father Al simply wanted the 1,200 battered souls within it, at whatever price. Soon Young's eyes lit up; he had grown weary of the priest who had become the perennial thorn in his side. He consented to the terms. One week before Jaesaengwon was to come under Father Al's control, though, Soon Young added a jumbo upfront cost. Father Al had to pull out.

The next day, Soon Young invited him back to Jaesaengwon under the pretense of renegotiations. Against his better judgment, Father Al stepped into his office, where Soon Young grabbed him by the throat and threatened his life. Lepers and gang members surrounded Father Al and began to beat him. They eventually threw

him into an adjoining room and locked the door. After some time,
Soon Young freed Father Al to continue the failed negotiations,
but the priest managed to break through the gauntlet and race back
to the Beggars' Hospice.

Two weeks later, when Father Al was jogging on an isolated road,
Soon Young passed him in his jeep, screeched to a halt, jumped out,
and attacked him. Father Al explained the scene in his journals:

> He tried to drag me into his jeep, but I resisted. Since he was much
> bigger and heavier than I, I was no match for him in a wrestling
> bout. As I was flopping around on the side of the road trying to get
> free, Big Daddy gave instructions to a passerby he knew to hurry to
> the Jaesaengwon and bring some help. After a while, I diverted Big
> Daddy's attention, broke loose, and ran. Big Daddy was stronger than
> I, but I was faster, and easily left him in my tracks. I jogged back to
> the convent by a side road. Somehow word had already reached the
> Sisters that Big Daddy was wrestling with me on the side of the road,
> and everyone was in a state of alarm.[9]

This attack came on the heels of Damiano being ambushed by a gang
of lepers. And the Sisters of Mary were sustaining daily threats each
time they stepped outside of the hospice.

With seemingly no relief in sight, Father Al gathered his humble
team of Commandos and devised a plan. They would work nonstop
to gather signatures of Busan residents eager to end the reign of the
city's most notorious gangster. Over the course of the next three
weeks, Sisters flooded the streets with clipboards, smiles, and a pen.
At the conclusion of the campaign, they had gathered more than
123,000 signatures. Their effort wasn't wasted; the signatures and
documentation of abuses were sent to the president of South Korea,
who initiated an undercover investigation of Soon Young and the
Jaesaengwon complex. Three months later, on June 1, 1971, Soon
Young was arrested and found guilty of violations of child welfare law, embezzlement, and acts of violence. He was given a five-
year suspended prison sentence. Each of his welfare businesses was
shut down.

[9] PM.

"People wonder why Fr. Al had to carry out a lonely fight against 'Big Daddy' for five years, with only the help of the valiant Sisters of Mary and a few staff members—and without any help from the church", Damiano wrote. "In *Poverty: Sign of Our Times* ... he made these suggestions to missionary priests: 'Do not seek peace at any price. For fear of rocking the boat, do not remain silent about injustice to the poor, even if the injustice is committed by the powers that are in the Church. Christ came to cast fire on the earth, and the fire of which he speaks is, primarily, justice.' "[10]

WHEN THE CITY CLOSED JAESAENGWON, a most beautiful event unfolded: hundreds of wobbly-kneed boys and girls were led by the Sisters of Mary from their valley of tears to the Beggars' Hospice across the street, a place the orphans had always peeked out their window to see as a humble castle at the top of a hill. No one knew it at the time, but the zig-zagging line of children making their way to the hospice became the dawn of perhaps the greatest movement of orphan care in the history of the world. Father Al suddenly found himself the custodian of more than seven hundred boys and more than one hundred girls. That summer day marked the beginning of Father Al's Boystown and Girlstown programs for the once-jailed teenage children; it began the moment the first Sister knelt down to take a broken child into her arms.

As the Sisters made room for the girls in one of their orphanages, Father Al lodged the boys in his newly constructed Amadong middle school. This would mark the beginning of the first unofficial Boystown and Girlstown—a name likely inspired by Father Flanagan's famous Boys Town community outside Omaha, Nebraska. Later that fall, he purchased nearby land and broke ground for the first official Boystown. Schwartz worked closely with the builder and the architect, instructing them to include a chapel, classrooms, dormitories, a gymnasium, a cafeteria, a large in-ground swimming pool, and playing fields. Like John Bosco, he wanted the boys to be boys. He knew that young men, caught up in a journey to wholeness and recovery, could more easily come to experience and understand the sacramental energy of the Catholic faith if their body and soul were

[10] Park, *Father Al, Who Is Still Alive*, 46–47.

both engaged. Like in the family-unit orphanages, the Sisters would act as mothers to these children, not teaching them classes, but guiding them, counseling them, playing sports with them, praying with them, loving them.

It is interesting to note that Father Al refused to slow down his priestly duties or his work for the poor during his long-haul struggles to beat back the storms of Bishop Choi and Soon Young. In 1970, he used Korean Relief donations to build his largest project to date, a 120-bed Sisters of Mary Hospital for the poor. It was the only hospital in the country that treated exclusively the abandoned sick and dying poor; all care was free. The new hospital was essential in relieving the strain placed on the medical teams at his three dispensaries, who were treating several hundreds of patients each day.

After learning of the success of Busan's Boystown program—and aware of the war he had to win against Soon Young to bring it to life—President Chung-hee sent government officials down from Seoul to implore Father Al to consider taking over management of a portion of the capital city's "City-Government Sponsored Camp", a prison-like facility that housed more than two thousand orphans. When Father Al visited a few weeks later, he paid witness to what seemed a bleak carbon copy of the old Beggars' Hospice before the takeover. Children stared at Damiano and Father Al with deadened eyes; they, too, had seemingly been abandoned by humanity. Father Al accepted the challenge, and within a year, he and the growing order of the Sisters of Mary had completely turned around the state ward.

Stunned by the resurrection of the facility, President Chung-hee invited Father Al to dinner at his residence, the Blue House. As Father Al sat across from the mayor, Seoul's superintendent of schools, and other government officials, Chung-hee asked the priest if he would consider breaking ground for a Boystown in Seoul. The next day, Father Al consulted with the Sisters of Mary community and explained details of the president's request. Each Sister agreed they would be willing to try. Several began making travel plans; it was time to spread the mission beyond the bounds of Busan.

Korea's second Boystown program opened on January 1, 1975, the Solemnity of Mary, the Mother of God. Father Al was now the guardian of more than three thousand children. Then in July 1978,

1944, St. Charles College, Catonsville, Maryland. Al Schwartz as a first-year minor seminarian, age fourteen.

Between 1944 and 1948, St. Charles College. Another photograph of Al.

1952. Al's passport photo, prior to leaving on a ship for Belgium for studies at the Louvain with the Société des Auxiliaires des Missions.

1953, Louvain, Belgium. Al's first year with the Société des Auxiliaires des Missions. He often biked through snow, rain, and ice to get to class.

1953, Grand Canyon du Verdon, France. Atop a mountain near Bauduen, France, during his summer with the country priest Abbé Duggot.

1965, Busan, South Korea. In front of his rectory in the poor neighborhood of Song-do.

Between 1961 and 1965, Busan, South Korea. Father Al lived in this "Pastor's Poorhouse" for five years, without running water, electricity, or plumbing.

1969, Busan, South Korea. Father Al washing a naked man with a gaping stomach wound at the once-notorious Beggars' Hospice, which was transformed by the Sisters of Mary.

1965, Busan, South Korea. Father Al with Bishop John Choi of Busan and children of the Amidong slum.

1969, Busan, South Korea. Orphans dining at a Sisters of Mary "family-unit" orphanage.

1977, Seoul, South Korea. Lunch for some of the two thousand orphans inside of Seoul's formerly prison-like "City-Government Sponsored Camp", which Father Al reformed.

1970, Busan, South Korea. Father Al tending to a resident with a serious head wound at the Beggars' Hospice.

1978, Busan, South Korea. Boystown, where thousands of abandoned children were given safe shelter, nourishment, and an introduction to family life.

1967, Busan, South Korea. Father Al laughing with an early group of professed Sisters by the shoreline of the Sea of Japan.

1977, Busan, South Korea. A "mother-sister" of a family unit praying the Rosary with her children. For several decades, children have prayed the Rosary together with the Sisters of Mary at seven P.M.

1982, Seoul, South Korea. The inauguration of George E. Doty Memorial Hospital, which Wall Street icon George Doty (in suit, tie) founded in honor of his deceased infant grandson, Brian Christopher Wert.

1988, Manila, Philippines. The gregarious Jaime Cardinal Sin, Archbishop of Manila, with Father Al at the inauguration of the Manila Girlstown.

1976, Busan, South Korea. Orphaned boys in front of their future seven-story Boystown home.

1978, Seoul, South Korea. Boystown elementary children enjoying a soccer match at their school.

1981, Seoul, South Korea. Father Al (center, hands crossed) with a group of men who would later become the Brothers of Christ, an order he founded to assist the work of the Sisters of Mary.

1981, Seoul, South Korea. Brother Ignatius Gu, a pioneer member of the Brothers of Christ, handing out fruit to a group of homeless men in Seoul.

1987, Busan, South Korea. Father Al with cheerful orphans.

1987, Busan, South Korea. Father Al boxing in the countryside with a resident of Boystown, ball cap cocked for effect.

1976, Busan, South Korea. More than five hundred boys joined Father Al for Boystown's first full-course marathon. Father Al ran every day of his priesthood, until ALS stopped him.

1976, Busan, South Korea. Surrounded by cheering students and Sisters of Mary nuns, Father Al crosses the finish line of a marathon.

1970, Seoul, South Korea. Sisters of Mary competing in a soccer match. Each day throughout the world, the Sisters of Mary play soccer, basketball, softball, and other sports with their students.

1980, Seoul, South Korea. A Sister of Mary minds the net on a penalty kick on a Seoul Boystown soccer pitch.

1977, Seoul, South Korea. Father Al standing before the building of another Boystown.

1981, Seoul, South Korea. Father Al with middle-school students at the completed Boystown.

1985, Manila, Philippines. "Smokey Mountain", the principal dumping site of Manila's trash, where thousands lived and scavenged for daily sustenance. Father Al's visit here would convince him to expand to the Philippines.

1985, Manila, Philippines. Sister Michaela Kim on Smokey Mountain. Many children were escorted from the mountain and became students at Boystowns and Girlstowns in Manila.

1985, Manila, Philippines. Father Al often visited with destitute families and children living within the debris on Smokey Mountain.

1986, Manila, Philippines. Father Al holding the set of blueprints for his first building in Manila—a home and school for more than one thousand poor children.

1991, Busan, South Korea. A pair of students at Boystown help Father Al—in the throes of ALS—to find his way down the stairwell to celebrate Mass in the chapel.

1992, Manila, Philippines. Sisters welcoming Father Al on his return from Mexico and Korea, just months prior to his death.

1992, Cavite, Philippines. The tomb of Father Al in Silang, Cavite, Philippines. "All praise, honor, glory, and thanksgiving to the Virgin of the Poor."

he launched the first official Girlstown in Busan. This growing family would become the future Catholic wave that spread throughout all of South Korea.

SISTER SOPHIA KIM, one of the original members of the religious community, said Father Al's efforts were all the more remarkable because of the indifference and apparent scorn the Korean Catholic hierarchy had for the wide-sweeping revitalization movement:

> He had saved more than one thousand children and adults detained in a concentration-camp-like institution [run by] a gangster.... [He continually faced] physical violence and legal suits. He saved more than one thousand orphaned children and one thousand homeless men maltreated in the Seoul City Institutions. At the beginning of our foundation, the diocese ... through their weekly bulletin, [told] each parish to not send candidates to the Sisters of Mary.... It was shocking news to us, who needed more hands to take care of the daily increasing number of people who needed our help.... In general [Father Al] was silent.... He wasn't afraid of them because he believed that God understood everything.[11]

In some sense, Father Al understood he would never be accepted by the Church establishment and his fellow clergy in South Korea. He was an American priest in a foreign land helping to rebuild a nation that wasn't his own. Moreover, he had seen how the money he had raised to resurrect welfare systems had made him vulnerable to whispers and subtle attacks, even from bishops. But because he was a priest who strove to emulate Christ in his voluntary poverty and concern for the poor, he simply did not care what others thought of him. He also knew it was due to those donations, and his and the Sisters' work, that many thousands of the poor, orphans, and marginalized were coming to the fullness of faith in the Catholic Church.

Throughout the Catholic renaissance for the poor in Korea, bishops and clergy had mostly shunned him or worked to delegitimize his work. Bishop Choi had provoked among the clergy widespread animus against Father Al. Triumphal achievements for the poor were made to be the overadventurous, vainglorious work of a lone wolf,

---

[11] *Pos,* 238–39.

an American cowboy. The bishop's calumnies oozed into chanceries and rectories throughout South Korea. Rumors of his so-called reckless pioneering spirit inspired six separate visitations from apostolic nuncios, one of whom gave Father Al some startling counsel. "He advised me with great seriousness that I should leave the priesthood and the Church", Father Al wrote in *Killing Me Softly*. "I pointed out that this was strong advice. His reply was a very eloquent shrug of the shoulders and he threw his hands up in the Italian gesture which says no explanation is really necessary."[12]

Still, just as he had achieved with Cardinal Agagianian in Rome, each of the furrow-browed nuncio's concerns was turned inside out by the staggering stories of grace and recovery that Father Al shared. He found that each visit concluded with approval: *You are doing much for the poor; onward.* The Italian-born nuncio living in Seoul who had suggested he leave the priesthood contacted him months later, asking if he could witness the work of the Sisters up close in Busan. So moved was the nuncio by the experience that he asked to celebrate Mass for them. He then confirmed more than 350 boys from Father Al's Boystown community. Before leaving, Father Al and the nuncio had lunch, "where we spoke as if we were lifelong buddies".[13] Father Al left the meal with rosaries, medallions, and pictures blessed by the newly installed Pope John Paul II.

Still, the Korean bishops' wholesale rejection of his mission for the poor was painful for Father Al. Only his Carmelite spiritual mother, Sister Gertrude, knew the impact his mental burdens and sorrow had on him. For more than three decades the pair traded handwritten letters sharing prayer requests, day-to-day minutiae, and the depths of their spiritual thought, and occasionally the habitually stoic American priest let his pain and lonesomeness speak. For example, Father Al wrote to her these words:

> It seems also that the more this work grows and the more recognition we get, the more the hostility of the local Korean hierarchy intensifies.... For almost 20 years now the Korean hierarchy has given us absolutely no support, morale, material, or otherwise. On the

---

[12] *KMS*, 58.
[13] *KMS*, 59.

contrary, they have opposed this work every inch of the way.... If this is the work of God—and to date, everything indicates that it is—it will continue, with or without the help of the Korean hierarchy....

I am always under extraordinary inner pressure with so many decisions, problems, responsibilities, and worries. I seem to wear an invisible "crown of thorns" which causes constant tension and mental pain. It is also the source of a very deep, spiritual "*unfelt*", and constant peace and joy. In other words, this "crown of thorns" is a grace and a privilege for which I never cease to give praise and gratitude.

But at times, one's courage wavers and falters.... Thus the need for constant prayer. Also, without prayer, there is the ever-present danger of self-deception and illusion. Under the pretense of seeking God's will and glory, it is so easy to be misled into seeking only one's self. Please pray for the grace that I may see clearly what God wants of me and [have] the courage to carry it out.[14]

Monsignor Golasinski, who traveled to Rome in the early 1970s in an urgent attempt to convince Vatican authorities of the threat Soon Young posed, said Father Al kept quiet about the deep sadness brought on by his persecutors. "I know he felt humiliated. There was a loneliness and discouragement that came from his rejection", Monsignor Golasinski recalled. "But I think that humiliation helped him become more like Christ. Father Al was very often completely alone, but that's what helped him become so close to the poor. He became alone, just like them."

This was the wilderness he had desired since his youth, the hunger to know the poverty of Christ. His Yes to Mary in Banneux brought him to it all.

---

[14] *DJ*, 34, 50.

12

Surging and Falling

Expansion to the Philippines and ALS, 1975–1989

BY THE MID-1980S, Father Al, at the age of fifty-five and still running up to six miles every day, saw—for once—only wide-open lanes in front of him. On a wintry night in January 1981, Soon Young and his second wife had been killed in a car accident. Bishop Choi had long ago receded into Father Al's past; the Holy See, on September 19, 1973, had asked for the Korean bishop's resignation. He was just sixty-one years old and hadn't planned to retire for fourteen more years, but Rome had other plans. The apostolic visits investigating Father Al's work had run their course, and the trouble from Korea's hierarchy and occasional gripes from American bishops had also mostly faded away. Since Father Al had arrived in Korea on the Feast of the Immaculate Conception in 1957, his path forward had never been this clear. In 1984, the same year Father Al was nominated for the Nobel Peace Prize, he seemed intent to create humble dwelling places of resurrection for every broken soul in Korea.

Newspaper stories about the cheery-faced nuns and the American priest—bringing light to many thousands of orphans, penniless men and women, unwed mothers, rejected elderly, mentally and physically disabled people, and the tubercular—began to spread across the globe. Indeed, the sheer scale of the work was breathtaking. Take just one day: on January 6, 1981, Father Al opened a new home for four hundred of Seoul's most severely developmentally disabled children, then a few hours later made his way across town to purchase and take management of a state-run camp for 1,800 homeless. But the articles on Father Al centered instead on his sacrifice, a man who had given himself entirely to the enfeebled. Reports on the Sisters of Mary caught the attention of tens of thousands, including Pope John Paul II, Ronald Reagan, and Mother Teresa. On Pope John Paul's papal visit to Korea in 1984, Stephen Cardinal Kim, who remained skeptical of Father Al throughout the 1970s and 1980s, discouraged the pontiff from visiting a Boystown or Girlstown, though it had been on his pre-trip itinerary. Yet the pope asked a helicopter pilot to circle the Busan Boystown, where hundreds of boys craned their necks and looked into the sky. They had no idea that the pope was giving them a special blessing from the hovering craft.

The Sisters of Mary, whose numbers had increased to above one hundred by the mid-1980s, had joined Mother Teresa's Missionaries of Charity as arguably one of the hardest-working orders in the world. They spilled into the streets before daybreak and came home when the first stars began to flicker. They devoted three hours of the day to prayer, where they implored God for the grace to help them persevere through often repulsive situations. Father Al had emphasized from their earliest days that it would only be because of their long periods of prayer and meditation that they could oblige tasks most others would never conceive of doing. As he made his rounds in Busan and Seoul, the Sisters often saw him disappear into chapels or isolated rooms to pray. He was frequently seen walking and praying the Rosary. "I would see him praying in the chapel on the fourth floor of the hospital [in Seoul] kneeling between the statue of Mary and the altar and he wouldn't make a single movement for an hour", Sister Marie Stella-Him said.

Because Father Al had observed how excess comfort deformed man's behavior, he taught the Sisters that *living poor* was sacrosanct. His amputation of comfort seemed to stir in them a like-minded desire to give all. They saw their spiritual father as a poor priest. His living quarters were small and contained only a narrow bed, a desk, and a chair. Besides his vestments and priestly garb, he owned only a few pairs of clothing and an emblem-less baseball cap. He wore the soles of his loafers and running shoes down until they disintegrated. He walked into meetings with land developers, engineers, architects, mayors, and city planners, to hash out multimillion-dollar projects, dressed in a threadbare shirt and pants. His cassock, when he wore it, was frayed at the bottom. Whenever friends, visiting family members, or benefactors offered to purchase him new clothes or shoes, he declined. "He lived poor and he died poor.... He had no vice", said Sister Teresita Prudente. "He was not attracted to the worldly, material, or physical pleasures."[1] On the wall of Father Al's bedroom was an old painting of "Ecce Homo"—Pilate bringing a scourged and battered Jesus before the crowds of Jerusalem—hung on a nail above his wood-framed bed.

Father Al wrote why the poor were often left abandoned, even by those who claim to serve them:

> It is so easy almost unconsciously to fall into the error of thinking that poverty is mostly statistics, facts, and figures. Poverty is more than this; it is above all *people*. Poverty has a human face and a human heart. True, its face is not always pretty to look at. And at times its heart, too, is badly scarred, even twisted. But until we get into the habit of looking poverty squarely in the face and seeing there the image of the Poorman of Nazareth we are approaching the problem in something less than a Christian manner.[2]

In the summer of 1981, he founded an all-male order—the Society of Christ—who would join the Sisters of Mary in centering their lives around embracing the rejected poor, the mentally unsound, and the tubercular. The community of men began working each day at Father Al's new "Village of Life Building", amid the stench of more than two thousand homeless men in Seoul. Quickly, though, the building became odorless, well-ordered, and calm. In November of the same year, he cut the ribbon for a brand-new middle school in Busan's slums. He followed the school opening by launching two new seven-story-high Boystown and Girlstown buildings in Busan and Seoul.

On a rainy day in 1984, Father Al wrote to Sister Gertrude about the breadth of his and the Sisters' work:

> The pouring rain makes me think of the graces which have been pouring down on us of late. More so than ever before. It is difficult to express—but none the less real.

[1] *Pos*, 170.
[2] *Pov*, photo insert.

My family of needy people continues to grow. Every day more and more children come to us. Our hospitals are almost overwhelmed by the ever-increasing number of patients who come begging for help. The number of people at the Kaengsaengwon [newly built home for Seoul's homeless] now exceeds 1,700 and continues to climb. The number of unwed mothers and newborn infants in our care continues to grow also.

I am planning more construction. All this, of course, means more headaches and more worries. But they are happy headaches and blessed worries—and I welcome them with joy.... I try to live day to day, following easily and lightly wheresoever the spirit leads. Pray for me.[3]

By the mid-1980s, Father Al was directing fifteen to twenty million dollars a year to homes, hospitals, and centers for the downtrodden. Still, he never kept a dollar on him, even when God began to send him men like George Doty.

DOTY WAS A NEW YORKER and daily Mass communicant who came into Father Al's life in the 1970s after he had made a large donation to memorialize his infant grandson Brian Christopher Wert, who had died of SIDS in his bassinet at his parents' temporary housing in Camp Casey, Seoul. Doty and his daughter, Anne Marie, traveled from America five years later to visit Brian's grave in the Korean capital. At some point in their travels, Doty met up with Father Al, where he began to sense he was in the presence of a special man, someone unlike anyone he had ever met. He accompanied Father Al to one of his Boystown sites and was stunned by what seemed a radiant indwelling of Catholicity, order, and sustained peace. Seeing the machine and mechanical shops, the classrooms that catered not only to science, math, and language, but to tailoring, cooking, and construction, Doty understood that Father Al was preparing the boys for life after five years of fully accredited schooling. After the visit, he sat Father Al down, and the echo of Gratian Meyer from two decades earlier came back—*Father, I think I can really help you.*

Father Al didn't know that the New Yorker was a Wall Street icon, the third-in-command at Goldman Sachs, one of the world's largest international investment firms. There were twenty-six Jewish

[3] *DJ*, 62–63.

partners, two Protestant Christians, and a single Catholic—Doty. His deft touch and conservative handling of investors' fortunes had brought him great wealth, but his aw-shucks decency and benevolence reminded most on Wall Street of George Bailey from *It's a Wonderful Life*. He struck everyone he met as a humble and kindly gentleman, a paragon of uncommon, unbendable virtue.

The Wall Street legend was also one of the most generous Catholic philanthropists in the world, a man who would one day financially spearhead the renovation of the Great Dome of the Church of the Holy Sepulchre in Jerusalem. Doty would eventually become the largest benefactor in the history of Korean Relief. Before Doty died in 2012 at the age of ninety-four, he had made more than 250 separate donations to Father Al's programs to the sum of forty-eight million dollars. And in his obituary, it was requested that in lieu of flowers mourners consider making donations to the Sisters of Mary. Brian Christopher, who died at five months, unwittingly helped tens of thousands of starving Koreans.

It was on the back of one of Doty's multimillion-dollar donations that Father Al built a 120-bed Sisters of Mary Hospital in Seoul in 1982, his second full-service hospital devoted entirely to the poor, later renamed the George E. Doty Memorial Hospital. Because Father Al was aware that surgeons and medical personnel might waver in committing day in and day out to the poverty-stricken, he paid them higher wages than other hospitals. Accordingly, his hospitals in Busan and Seoul boasted several of Korea's top surgeons and brightest medical minds. Father Al was firm with builders and architects at the beginning stages of new projects: he demanded they spare no expense for the poor.

Edsel Ledesma, the engineer and contractor Father Al had hired to build his shelters and hospitals in the 1980s, said that a nearby order of priests, the Fathers of La Salette, thought Father Al was a beggar. The "beggar" repeatedly told Ledesma to create solid and lasting structures. He said that the poor and the orphan should feel the warmth and safety of a sturdy dwelling place.

"To the children he took under his and the Sisters' care, he had what seemed inexhaustible generosity. He spared nothing", Ledesma reported. "'Top-notch' and 'the best available in the market' were Father Al's main specifications for all equipment during the design and specification stages of the dormitories and classroom for the children." The engineer continued, " 'Fr. Al,' the designer would bargain, 'these children are squatters and from the dumpsites. We don't need first-class equipment for them. We could save on costs.' To which Fr. Al would retort, 'The poorest of the poor deserve only the best.' "[4]

A MARYLAND MAN, Tom Sullivan, returned from work one evening and, as was his custom, read from the evening *Washington Star* after dinner. His eyes were drawn to a photograph of a full-habited nun minding the net as a goalkeeper in a soccer game, which elicited memories of playing soccer with his Sisters of St. Joseph teachers in Saint Louis. He read the article and called the reporter, William Willoughby, whom he invited to dinner the following night. Tom and his wife, Glory, peppered him with questions about Father Al, the Sisters, and all that he had experienced on the recent trip he had taken to Korea. Willoughby told them that he had witnessed the work of a saint. The next day, Tom and Glory sent the first of what would become hundreds of checks in the mail to Father Al.

In time, the Sullivans began to direct ten percent of their prosperous environmental publishing firm's pretax income to the mission. In appreciation of their generosity, Father Al, who returned to America to make a retreat in the early 1980s, stopped by their home for dinner. Glory Sullivan said she expected a man built like a giant and was stunned when she opened the front door:

> Here's a man five foot seven, 130 pounds soaking wet. I'll never forget that night. We had met a man unlike anyone we had ever known or ever would know. It was a Thursday night, a school night, and after dinner our three kids gathered at his feet. They sat mesmerized by what he was doing in Korea. He had this way of holiness to him. They couldn't get over how he was taking care of thousands and thousands of children—they kept asking him for more stories and he kept answering them. They didn't want him to leave. Finally, after it was late and it was time for the kids to get upstairs for bed, we let Father Al out. We closed the door, and Tom and I looked at each other and said, simultaneously, "We have just met a saint."

[4] *FA*, 90.

Willoughby, the reporter, had written of Father Al:

None of us will live long enough to realize it, but a couple of hundred years from now would you believe that Washington D.C., yes Washington D.C., is going to have its first native son canonized a saint? ... [Father Al] would cringe if he knew I was writing it. But I honestly think I know a saint in the works when I see one.

Undoubtedly South Korea knows it is entertaining a modern-day saint, a man who aches with every ache that the poor and hungry and the dying in the slums of Seoul and Busan ache daily. He and a number of hardworking, unheralded nuns and doctors are laboring around the clock to show the love of God to kids, many of whom have never known what it is to have a home or a real solid meal, let alone someone to love them.[5]

Willoughby wrote of the Sisters of Mary in a later article:

You can hardly believe your eyes. You've never seen a smile until you see theirs. I saw Christ in every one of them. Christ giving the kids a bath. Christ mending their clothes. Christ watching over the cares and the antics of the mentally retarded. Christ washing the wounds. Christ washing away tears.

And Christ playing soccer with the kids. They actually get out and play soccer with the boys more than Father Schwartz does.... And the whole country is catching marathon fever. Schwartz has everyone running, including the nuns. Several of them plan to enter the next regional and national competition, running the full 26 miles.... They're gunning to beat Al Schwartz, who at 47, is a running nut.[6]

ON AUGUST 30, 1983, Father Al became the first foreigner to be awarded the Ramon Magsaysay Award for International Understanding, the Asian equivalent of the Nobel Peace Prize, sponsored by the government of the Philippines. Cardinals, bishops, dignitaries, and foreign leaders flew into Manila from all parts of the Far East to honor Father Al, who was both embarrassed and humbled by the

---

[5] Willoughby, "Running with Washington's Saint in the Making", *Washington Star*, July 16, 1977.

[6] Willoughby, "Here's a Hard Man (and Gals) to Keep Up With", *Washington Star*, July 15, 1978.

distinction. One attendee, Jaime Cardinal Sin, was a larger-than-life-sized, happy-faced cardinal from the host country. Cardinal Sin was known for opening the door of his chancery and welcoming guests by dramatically sweeping his red cape and bellowing in the accent of Count Dracula, "*Vell*-come ... to the House of Sin!"

The gregarious cardinal needed a lift on the evening Father Al's plane touched down in Manila. Prominent Filipino Senator Benigno Aquino Jr., a vocal opponent of President Ferdinand Marcos, had been assassinated on the tarmac of the Manila International Airport just a week prior. Cardinal Sin's soul was troubled by the anger and violence that was already beginning to spread onto Manila's streets. Amid the congratulatory throng that evening, a visibly moved Cardinal Sin approached Father Al and got to the point: "Father, I need you and your sisters in my country."

Three weeks later, Father Al made a return trip to the Philippines, where Cardinal Sin and he drove out to the nation's most tragic landmark, Smokey Mountain. Several miles before reaching their destination, Father Al began to breathe in a noxious stench and watch an ethereal haze slowly lift from the mountain, like the incense of the dead. As they arrived at its base, Father Al saw that beneath the mist was a mass of humanity moving to and fro, like the gyration of maggots in a dead robin. Cardinal Sin explained that he was beholding the souls of more than twenty thousand Filipino mountain dwellers who spent their days rooting through oceanic fields of smoldering garbage dumped by Manila's sanitation department throughout the day. As they walked the narrow lanes formed by walls of trash, Father Al saw swarms of flies covering the stooped scavengers. It was a heartbreaking scene, unlike any he had encountered.

Hundreds of children, too, were scattered about, picking through the heaps; many were emaciated, naked, and caked in grime and sweat. Father Al saw they were risking puncturing their fingers and toes on shattered window panes, shards of glass, and rusted nails hidden within in the sea of debris.

The pitiful scene, though—paradoxically—brought Father Al hope. The children weren't surrendering to circumstance; he saw a bursting forth of energy in those who wouldn't give in to the indignities swallowing their life. He saw that wonder still shone in their eyes. As Christ wept as he turned to Jerusalem, Father Al shed tears over the children's potential. These children—as many as he could get to—would receive their release.

Father Al didn't share his thoughts with Cardinal Sin at the time, but perhaps he knew he was looking at some of the future students of the Philippines Boystown and Girlstown programs. These souls, who had never felt the flow of running water, flushed a toilet, or turned on a light switch—or even slept in a bed or turned the page of a book—would be the future electricians, plumbers, architects, teachers, and orchestral musicians of the Philippines. He also perhaps knew, in God's incomprehensible way, there were likely a few future priests and sisters hidden amid the trash. The majority of the children would be the first in generations to graduate with a high school diploma. These were the modern-day lepers whom the Sisters and he would soon embrace.

Father Al wrote to Sister Gertrude after he visited Smokey Mountain: "I spent ten days there. Days of rich grace and intense anguish. The poverty and destitution is overwhelming, and grows worse with each passing day. After much thought, prayer, advice, and sweating of blood, I have made my decision. Yes, I will give it a try."[7]

On August 15, 1985, Father Al began his first center for care at Manila's most deplorable social welfare hospital, the wretched state-run Quezon Tuberculosis Hospital. Quezon's exterior resembled a horror house; the interior—where more than eight hundred patients resided—was just as macabre. Before the Sisters of Mary took over, as many as three patients shared a bed, while others spent the day on the floor. Many patients sold their prescriptions to drug dealers.

Father Al started his work by redesigning and renovating large portions of its enormous interior. He then gained control of medication disbursements and asked the Sisters to cater to each patient on an individual basis. A chapel was built; new X-ray machines, beds, and medical equipment were brought in; and a full-time chaplain was installed to administer the sacraments, celebrate daily Mass, and chat with the patients each day. Eventually, a new team of doctors and medical staff was installed—and within a year, the staff was treating more than 2,300 inpatients and outpatients each day. Young Filipina postulants and novices in the Sisters of Mary spent time with

[7] DJ, 60

patients every day. "If not for the guidance of the Sisters of Mary, I wouldn't have learned how to pray", said Sofio Bustamante, a tubercular patient at Quezon. "And without them I would have probably died."[8] Father Al redubbed it the Quezon Institute.

In 1986, Father Al inaugurated a Boystown and Girlstown for a total of more than three thousand Filipino students, some of whom Sisters brought down from Smokey Mountain. Those who had once never bathed now had a large in-ground swimming pool; those who had pulled their meals from rotting debris now had three nutritious meals every day. Calloused, punctured fingers were now thumbing rosaries and flipping the pages of textbooks.

There is a remarkable before-and-after photograph of a young Filipina girl named Analyn de Vera. In the first photo, taken in 1988, she is seen sitting on the step of her family's hovel on Smokey Mountain. She seems curled into her grief and poverty; her eyes are empty wells of melancholy. In the second photo, taken two years later after her admittance into Girlstown, her smile is radiant, her face full, her eyes merry. She looks like an entirely different person.

Generous benefactors from Germany, Switzerland, England, and other European countries had joined American donors in spreading Father Al's new mission throughout the Philippines. He built two more seven-story-high Boystown and Girlstown centers in Talisay, on the overcrowded island of Cebu, and later built identical Boystowns and Girlstowns in the cities of Silang and Minglanilla. In total, the Sisters of Mary were caring for more than twelve thousand Filipino children at four different locations by the mid-1990s.

Because he had the eyes and practical-mindedness of John Bosco and saw that his high school sports teams had begun to win national championships, Father Al asked architects to build larger gymnasiums, with more outdoor basketball courts, soccer fields, indoor swimming pools, and larger tracks. Malnourished children who once plowed fields barefoot, who hadn't known the location of their next meal, were now some of the strongest, most athletic teenagers in Korea and the Philippines. Some of their soccer teams never lost games and were playing on a national stage before crowds that reached the thousands. There are dozens of photographs of Boystown and Girlstown

[8] *Pos*, 164

sports teams standing in front of national championship trophies the size of washing machines. One graduate, Kim Byung-ji, would go on to become one of the greatest soccer players in the history of Korea.

Boystown and Girlstown string orchestras began to win national competitions and were invited to play at Carnegie Hall and celebrated concert halls throughout the Far East. High school graduates from Father Al's schools were accepting jobs at Proctor and Gamble, Toyota, Samsung, Nissan, and dozens of other established companies throughout Asia. Thousands of others left for college or pursued master's degrees and doctorates. Many gave their lives over to Christ and joined the women who formed them, the Sisters of Mary. The Catholic faith was spreading throughout all of Korea through resurrected, catechized youth. "[What Father Al did with the Boystowns and Girlstowns] undoubtedly is beyond the human endeavor. It took the hand of God", remarked Filipino Bishop Manuel C. Sobrevinas.

Father Al celebrated the weddings of graduates and often was asked a year or two later to baptize the couple's newborn. In wedding homilies, he reminded all newly married couples that the key to a healthy marriage was their daily recitation of the Rosary.

In 1989, Father Al and the Sisters were providing sustenance and spiritual care for more than twenty thousand souls. He had established an effective system of travel, shuttling back and forth between Korea and the Philippines every two months, where he made it a point to visit each of his houses of care. He was hearing one to two hundred confessions a day, giving retreats to the Sisters and children, and spearheading new construction projects. His obligations and burdens were multitudinous, but he felt a sustained profusion of God's graces. He felt Our Lady of Banneux very close to him; he felt she was orchestrating everything through him and the Sisters. Although his daily schedule, tasks, building projects, and spiritual demands wearied him, he seemed eager to do far more for Mary and the poor. He shared his thoughts in a letter to Sister Gertrude in January 1989:

> These last six or seven weeks have been unbelievably busy. Even hectic. At times my poor head feels like a volcano ready to explode and spew out a thousand problems, plans, worries, concerns, and cares.
>
> But underneath the volcano flows a river of peace, which keeps my head cool, light, and full of peace. With St. Paul, I like to say: "I

am the slave of Christ". I ask him to remove from my breast my own freedom which I thoroughly distrust, and in its place to put his Spirit, His Will, His Heart, His glorious freedom....

Can I handle all this? No, not really. But I entrust all these plans and projects to the Virgin of the Poor. If it is for the glory of God, she will handle it quite well. The Virgin of the Poor, no matter how much money I use, continues to send me more. I feel that this is an indication that I should continue to expand. So many risks are involved, but I think we should try.

Also, I feel a sense of urgency. We are fighting for immortal souls. The devil does not sit still. He goes about like a roaring lion. I think we must move faster and roar even more loudly, if we wish to defeat him.

My health is never very good. Nothing comes easy. Every day is a struggle.[9]

For all his energy and enthusiasm, however, something was gnawing at him. He had emptied his heart and shared his inner turmoil in another letter to Sister Gertrude, written a few months earlier on November 26, 1988:

I am not afraid of making decisions and moving ahead. But I distrust myself and my own judgment, and I am deathly afraid of making decisions that are not in accordance with the will of my Father. It is such a precious grace to discern, discover, and decide what is His eternal, holy, and fruitful Will. This grace is so precious that it is not lightly given. One must be willing to enter the darkness, press his face to the earth, sweat and bleed and agonize. Then in good time, an angel comes and gives the necessary light. It is so good to doubt self and be always a bit uncertain and searching. It tends to keep one's heart humble and little....

Lately, there has been an avalanche of grace. At times I feel that I am buried under it, even crushed by it. But it is a very happy situation and I am most grateful.

Yes, for many years I have felt that St. Thérèse is truly a 'Soeur de mon âme' [soul mate]. (I hope that does not sound too pretentious.) Her presence in my life is very real, and her influence is felt daily.

Lately, in prayer, I look up and see rising before me a lofty mountain, whose peak is lost in the clouds. Jesus is on the peak, and He

[9] DJ, 146–47.

beckons me to climb. I feel that I am just beginning. The peak is so high, and the mountain seems so fierce and threatening that it frightens me. It speaks of tremendous sacrifice, suffering, pain.... But I do want to climb the mountain and reach the peak before I die—because this is what Jesus wants. So I will try, I will try my best.[10]

THE LETTER WAS PROPHETIC. Shortly after writing it, in July 1989, Father Al awakened in the middle of the night with his right arm trembling. The strange movement didn't stop until the morning. "Something serious was taking place in my body", he said.[11]

Later that year, on his trip back to Washington to make a retreat with the Carmelites, he shared the changes that were happening in his body with a Washington neurologist named Dr. Marvin Korengold. After several tests, Dr. Korengold told Father Al he likely had amyotrophic lateral sclerosis (ALS).

"I asked, 'Is the disease life-threatening?' He answered, 'Yes, it is. The usual period of time is three years.' "[12]

After the startling diagnosis, he returned to the Discalced Carmelite friars' monastery in Washington, D.C., where he had been staying. He fell into an intense period of prayer and contemplation; the three weeks at the monastery marked the longest amount of time he had ever spent away from his programs. He took light runs each day at the large nearby cemetery, which was cloaked with golden-branched trees and fallen autumn leaves. He wrote of that time:

> It was such a beautiful, even mystical experience that it is difficult to describe. The beauty, the silence, the softness, the solitude, and the presence of the dead, all created an atmosphere extremely conducive to contemplation. As I ran along the roads, looking at the tombs and the trees and the light and the beautiful sky, I thought of death, not in a morbid manner, but with a certain calm, serenity, and even joy. In my heart, I felt that these were my last runs.[13]

One night as he was preparing for sleep in his darkened bedroom, he suddenly lost his balance and began to fall to the ground. As he

---

[10] *DJ*, 143–44.
[11] *KMS*, 19.
[12] *KMS*, 27.
[13] *KMS*, 29.

reached out to cushion his fall, he mistakenly pried open a small panel that was attached to a bedroom wall. He didn't realize it at the time, but the fall was triggered by his worsening ALS.

As he lay on the ground, he was stunned by what the panel revealed. He saw it as the hand of God's providence, an indication of the Calvary that awaited him but also that he wouldn't be left alone throughout it:

> I was lying on the floor looking through a plate glass window at the chapel; below. The chapel was darkened. I could see the vigil light flickering and could see distinctly the altar and the tabernacle. I had not known it but the Fathers put me in a room reserved for sick patients. During Mass, the panel is opened and the priest staying in the room can assist at Mass and adore the Blessed Sacrament from his sick room.
>
> I lay on the floor a bit shaken and bruised, looking at the chapel, the flickering red light, and the tabernacle glowing in the soft light. I said to myself, "*Sacerdos et Victima*, Priest and Victim." This was Jesus. This was the call of the alter Christus. So I said in my heart, "Lord, if this is what you want, here I am. I offer myself as a victim to your Love."
>
> I knew St. Thérèse had offered herself as a victim to Divine Love and encouraged many "little souls" to follow her example. I took this occasion to mouth these words and speak this prayer, not fully realizing the implication of what I was saying. If at that time I knew what lay ahead, I am not sure I would have spoken these words so easily and so swiftly.[14]

A few days before leaving for the Far East, Father Al visited another Carmelite monastery; he wanted to spend time with discalced nuns in the countryside of Maryland, where he begged their prayers for his health and work. Knowing his visit with the community would likely be his last, he offered to celebrate a Mass for them. Sister Miriam of the Cross and other Carmelites, aware of the many tasks he had to get in order to prepare for his trip back to Korea, told him his gesture wasn't necessary. Father Al insisted. Sister Miriam—who like the other nuns knew nothing at the time of his ALS diagnosis—spoke years later of how moved she was by Father Al's display of sanctity at the Mass:

---

[14] *KMS*, 30.

He would not hear of [not celebrating Mass]. Finally with that nervous intensity that characterized him, he raced to the chapel. I expected him to say Mass hurriedly and briefly, as by then he was seriously late for his next appointment. However, to my surprise, he took time in the sacristy to place himself in the presence of God. Then he said one of the most beautiful Masses that I have ever attended. Time was no more. He was in the presence of God....

He said Mass as if it were his last, as indeed it was at this altar. I cannot begin to say adequately how much that impressed me, and of how I and the others present were drawn into his adoration and calm. From that moment, I thought of Father Schwartz as a saint.[15]

Aware that his body was weakening and his time on earth was limited, a thought churned in Father Al's head on his long journey home. He would ask the Sisters their thoughts on expanding and spreading the mission. And it was Mexico that kept coming to mind. Specifically, it was the Virgin of the Poor, who had changed form. No longer in white, the Virgin was now clothed with the sun, and stars were thrown about her turquoise mantle.

[15] *Pos*, 295–96.

13

Calvary

Mexico, Death, and Joy, 1989–1992

EARLY ONE MORNING IN 1989, before Father Al journeyed back to
the other side of the globe, someone knocked on his bedroom door
at the Carmelite monastery where he was temporarily staying. He
had been praying and preparing his soul for a day of contemplation
after just learning of his terminal disease. The visitor was a Carmelite priest who had seen Father Al at weekday Masses and passing
through monastery hallways. The priest apologized for the intrusion
and explained that the Holy Spirit had led him to Father Al's room.

The priest then poured out his heart and explained his eagerness
to build a "Carmelite City" on a mountain in his Venezuelan homeland. The poverty in Caracas and the surrounding slums had grown
too mighty even for Mother Teresa and her order to handle. The
poor needed prayerful and willing Carmelites to come down from
the mountain and aid the poor. After listening to the priest's "deep
faith, sincerity, and apostolic zeal", Father Al shared that he had built
similar homes of Catholic restoration on the other side of the world.
At the priest's urging, Father Al explained the origin of the Sisters of
Mary and of his Catholic-based schools, orphanages, hospitals, and
rehabilitation centers he had built in the slums of Korea and the Philippines. He told the priest of the new generations of strong Catholics
being formed and moving into cities, countrysides, workplaces, and
universities. The Carmelite's eyes widened. "Father, will you bring
these Boystowns and Girlstowns to Venezuela? So many are poor and
so many are leaving the faith."

Father Al considered the Carmelite's plea on his trip back to Korea, but in endeavoring to wrap his mind around an expansion to Venezuela, his thoughts traveled instead to Mexico, which he considered the gateway to poverty in Latin America. Perhaps God would one day lead the Sisters of Mary to Venezuela or someplace else in South America, but Father Al knew that if he was going to bring Boystowns and Girlstowns into the Western Hemisphere, he would bring them first to Mexico. Within the nightmare of his disease, the Virgin of the Poor, as Our Lady of Guadalupe, beckoned him to the land of her apparition, and he couldn't get it out of his head.

Back in Korea, though, he set all his thoughts of Mexico aside to tell his religious community about his diagnosis of ALS. And Sister Gertrude was one of the very first he told, via letter:

Among friends, there should be no secrets. While in the U.S. I had a medical check-up and it seems I have a number of problems. Fact is, I have been hurting, aching, and ailing nearly all of my life. I try not to pay much attention to it....

But the medical exams (very, very extensive) revealed that the problems are a bit more serious than I had originally thought. First of all, I have bad arthritis in the shoulder and hip.... But further neurological tests revealed that I have a disease of the nervous system called Amyotrophic Lateral Sclerosis—ALS! Amazing! The disease has my name on it....

There is no cure.... Realistically, I must plan as if I have only 3 years left—and during that time my health and strength will deteriorate. So you see, it is possible that I will arrive at our Father's house before you. This is in fitting with my character—always in a hurry, always wanting to be first.

What am I thinking of these days? This may sound crazy—and it probably is!—but I am thinking of trying to get our Boystown-Girlstown Program started in Latin America. Maybe Mexico. Maybe Venezuela. Maybe both.... But I have little time. Maybe I will give it a try. St. Teresa of Avila was dying when she founded her last convent.

Please pray to St. Thérèse of Lisieux and Bl. Teresa of Chile O.C.D. for this intention. Pray that I may have the light to see His Holy Will and the strength to accomplish it. This is the one grace necessary.[1]

[1] *DJ*, 156–57.

Because his communities were scattered over many hundreds of miles, it took Father Al a few weeks of travel to share the news of his neurological disease with all the Sisters of Mary, many of whom reacted with tears or stunned silence. He smiled cheerfully and showed a brave face as he explained the diagnosis, and he told each Sister that it was no time for sentimentalism or worry. In God's strange providence, he said, good would come and his holy will regarding their work would be done. As was Father Al's custom, he was plainspoken about the disease named after an old American baseball hero, Lou Gehrig. He told the Sisters they would begin to see his body betray him and that he would lose control over most of his bodily functions within two years. As his body withered, he would demand more of their attention, just like those, he noted, in their shelters for the tubercular. He would be like the leper on whom Jesus laid his hands, and he told them he would need their hands. In all likelihood, he informed them, he would be dead within three years.

Father Al's thousands of students at Boystowns and Girlstowns began to notice something was wrong with him. They looked outside classroom windows and saw that his jogs around their oval tracks were slower and somewhat hobbled. At Mass and in the confessional, children wondered why Father Al's voice was gravelly and occasionally slurred. He had become a wisp of a man; the black pants and shirts he wore flapped in passing breezes. Confused students, who shyly asked the Sisters about Father Al's changing appearance, often saw tears well in the Sisters' eyes. The children didn't know their spiritual father was dying before them and that throughout his jogs he was asking God to care for them after he was gone.

Despite his weakened state, no one in the Philippines or Korea saw him relent in the duties of his priesthood or his daily work. He still celebrated as many as three Masses a day and squeezed in as many as one hundred confessions. Most everyone from that time agreed he was working with even greater urgency. Knowing his remaining days couldn't be deprived of their source of power, he armed himself with even greater measures of prayer and with contemplation of the martyrs and contemplative saints. "He was inspired by Saint John Vianney", said Sister Elena Belarmino, who worked closely at that time with Father Al at the Quezon Institute. "Vianney said, 'In this world, we work, and in the next, we rest.' Father Al never stopped his mission, even when he was very sick. . . . All of his activities then were for the glory of God. He forgot his pains, sufferings, and difficulties and offered them to God."

Sister Elena remembered how his dedication affected her: "For me then, seeing Father Al very sick and still always awakening on time, preparing every day for [the Sisters'] meditation and Mass, then teaching us our classes, and observing the rest of his regular schedule with the poor—I can only say that it was heroic and holy. He forgot himself. He gave himself to God to save souls. In my mind, then, I was thinking, 'This is not Father Al who is doing it; it is God doing it in him.'"

In the winter of 1990, Father Al felt "off" as he vested and prepared for the celebration of Mass at the Sisters of Mary annual retreat and renewal of vows. After kissing the altar, he blessed himself and greeted the Sisters in a hoarse voice. To his horror, as he recited the Kyrie Eleison, he realized he had lost his voice. What he was able to articulate was barely comprehensible. He wasn't certain if the sudden loss of vocal function was due to an approaching illness or the dawn of ALS's assault on his vocal cords. As he stood helplessly at the altar, he noticed a priest at the back of the chapel and motioned for him to approach. He asked the startled priest in a whisper if he would vest and take his place on the altar. The priest obliged and rushed into the sacristy. In the interlude, Father Al looked awkwardly into the pews and saw that dozens of Sisters were crying.

As Father Al settled his nerves after Mass, he considered the incident as God's confirmation that he was too enfeebled to begin a mission in Latin America. His idea of expanding, he thought then, was not only imprudent and ill-conceived; it was unfeasible. Later in the day, he shared with a handful of Sisters who had attended the interrupted Mass that the Mexico idea was to be abandoned. He told them God had revealed his will by showing him his own weakness. Simply, Father Al said, there were too many roadblocks for serious consideration of expansion. He was shaken by their response:

> They countered, "How do you know, Father, that this was not simply a tactic of the devil to mislead you?" I wanted them to reassure me and help me to abandon the Mexican venture. Here they were, however, sowing more doubt and taking the opposite tack. The heart of the matter was I really did not know for sure, one way or the other, what the Lord wanted.

About this time, I received an invitation from Archbishop Dias, the Apostolic Nuncio and very good friend and long-time confidant of mine, to dine with him at the Nunciature. I spoke to him about the Mexican project and sought his advice. Being of clear mind and sound judgment, I felt that he would certainly advise against it. Once again, I was totally mistaken.

He urged me, very strongly and enthusiastically, to go ahead with the project. He said, "You begin it but you do not have to finish it. Others will do that. This will be your unfinished symphony."[2]

As Father Al began ploddingly to re-center his prayer and conversations with the Sisters around the possibility of expansion, Cardinal Sin surprised him one day—he was elevating him to honorary prelate, giving him the title of "monsignor". The cardinal wanted to pay tribute to Father Al's selfless priesthood and honor him for the astonishing volume of his work for the poor. Father Al immediately fought to decline the new designation, but his affable friend merrily roared that a rejection would be a breaking of the vow of obedience. The investiture ceremony, held at the Girlstown community in Manila, was attended by nineteen cardinals and bishops, dozens of prelates, an apostolic delegate, a sea of Sisters of Mary nuns, and a few thousand students and infirm. Father Al didn't tell any of the Mass attendees that he had awakened that morning fearing a collapse on the altar. He also worried that his declining voice might fall into a raspy whisper.

He had chosen to celebrate his investiture with the votive Mass of the Precious Blood, on February 1, 1990. Father Al wore a striking scarlet robe, paid for and given to him by Cardinal Sin for the Mass. As he wore his shoulder-to-shoe-top red satin vestment, his thoughts turned poetically to the blood-stained Christ, as well as to the many attacks he himself had sustained over the years, spiritual and physical. Dozens of his brethren despised him. His body, a thorn in his side since Louvain, was now finally collapsing. As he spoke, he understood he was fading away:

I mentioned that the priest, not just the Monsignor, was another Christ, and the color red was a reminder that as Christ, he was also priest and victim. The priest was called to mingle his blood with that

[2] *KMS*, 49.

of Christ to redeem the world and, to borrow a phrase from St. Paul, "to make up in his own flesh the sufferings lacking to the body of Christ." As I stood on the platform during Mass with my red robes and later the red vestments, I felt very much like Jesus. And I thought of the Ecce Homo pictures where Jesus is covered with blood and he wore this as a red robe of blood and humiliation. Deep inside I had a foreboding that this was the future that awaited me. During Mass, I prayed for patience, courage, and the determination to be faithful to Jesus until the end.[3]

As spring moved to summer, the expansion to the Western Hemisphere had become an abiding burr in Father Al's thoughts. Finally, he decided to leave for Mexico, where he would arrange to visit poor communities outside the capital of Mexico City. His first stop would be to the cavernous Shrine of Our Lady of Guadalupe, where he would lay his uncertainties at Mary's feet and beg for mystical clarity. He shared with the Sisters his plan. They listened "with open minds and courageous hearts.... Their only reservation was with my health. But outside of that, in essence, they said, 'Wherever you go, Father, we will follow.'"[4]

On a September morning in 1990, he joined with hundreds of other peasant worshippers at the shrine of the tilma, where he begged Mary for insight. He told her he was terrified of going against her Son's will. After praying, he considered the stakes:

I have little money, few people to assist me, no one on my team who has any knowledge of Spanish. To get started in Mexico City, I will need to find a large piece of land, get permission from the government and Church authorities, set up non-profit corporations, open bank accounts, contact builders we can trust, and recruit Mexican candidates willing to join and work with the sisters. Also, and perhaps most importantly, the total concept of our Boystown and Girlstown is very new, original and unorthodox. Would the parents of poor children buy the idea, in a word, would it work in Mexico? Deep inside I felt that the Apostolic Nuncio [who proposed the Mexican "unfinished symphony"] did not have a full understanding of what was involved here.[5]

[3] KMS, 61.
[4] KMS, 47.
[5] KMS, 50.

When meeting poor folks in the countryside, Father Al saw poverty that spoke differently to him than what he had confronted in Korea and the Philippines. He met with a handful of Mexican families he learned had abandoned the Catholic faith. Some had pivoted their worship to the evangelical churches that were spreading throughout Mexico's wide expanse. Others joined traditional Protestant churches. Many seemed to have left God altogether. This abandonment from God, he knew, was what led to the brokenhearted revolt in Banneux in the 1930s, when jobless fathers and overwrought mothers gave cold shoulder to the Sunday morning peal of bells at their tiny countryside parish. Countless poor Mexican children, Father Al knew, were being raised each day as orphans of the Catholic Church. Numberless homes weren't praying Rosaries at night—the daily custom of thousands of children at his Boystowns and Girlstowns on the other side of the world.

He wrote down his thoughts later:

> The Church in Mexico was being decimated. Especially, the Church was losing many of the poor, uneducated and the lowly—the very ones who have priority in the work of salvation....
>
> These children are a marvelous to-date untapped and undiscovered spiritual resource. Our goal is to turn them into lay apostles and to make them witnesses for the new, rejuvenated Church. These children will be the future elite for Christ and the Church and will help to stop the terrible spiritual hemorrhaging which is taking place in the Church of Mexico.[6]

Although his inner instincts screamed for him to commit to Mexico, he wouldn't do it. The cost of building new Boystown and Girlstown communities was exorbitant, and he had already committed several million dollars to ongoing and future Boystowns and Girlstowns and other projects in the Philippines. Two other Filipino bishops requested that he bring his programs to their own diocese. Another lingering thought plagued him, of course—he was dying. In a sense, he had become like Graham Greene's "whisky priest" in *The Power and the Glory*, an agonized, haunted man surrounded by the thousands of the poor who needed him but crippled by his own weakness. The prospect of his fading body taking on the money,

[6] KMS, 53–54.

management, and time necessary for a new mission seemed to him foolhardy at best, and absurd at worst.

As the Sisters had warned, Father Al knew his fears could be the cunning of the Evil One, but as his body weakened, a weed of indecisiveness rooted within him. Fighting off demons of worry wasn't as easy as it once had been. Mary's consoling voice had gone silent. His hero Vincent Lebbe, too, gave no answer. Doors that had always swung open for him now remained closed. He could not hear God. He didn't feel like a Boy Commando anymore. For the first time since his bodily collapse in 1958, he felt wearied.

In his confusion, as was his custom, Father Al turned his heart to the bold and suffering saints, those who also may have wavered in taking on sea-change movements. He considered Joan of Arc, John Bosco, Teresa of Avila, and Catherine of Siena. In his darkness, he turned to John of the Cross. "I was very much like a child in the night, a child crying for the light, with no other voice but a cry", he wrote.[7]

Finally, one bold Mexican priest of the Guadalupe Fathers challenged Father Al on his tentativeness: "Father, remember, still waters become stagnant and polluted; whereas running waters always remain fresh, clear, and vibrant."[8] After the subtle rebuke, Father Al vowed to make a decision on Mexico before returning home. In a past homily, he had preached about the measures one needed to take when crippled by fear:

> You must do violence ... to your instincts. Most people give up and turn back because they lack courage. This life of sacrifice, this life of self-discipline, self-violence is very difficult. It is very painful. It frightens us.... You are called to be mountain climbers, spiritual mountain climbers. It requires great courage, great sacrifice, and great self-discipline.[9]

Before leaving Mexico, a memory from Al's boyhood came to mind. He saw himself standing on a diving board on a sun-splashed afternoon in the summer of 1940. He was at a swimming pool not

[7] *KMS*, 48 (quotation marks omitted).
[8] *KMS*, 54.
[9] *Glow*, 49–50.

too far from his hard-luck home on Gales Street. No one in Washington, D.C., he felt, stood closer to the sky than he did that day, on one of the highest diving boards in the city. He explained the situation in *Killing Me Softly*:

> It was a matter of honor to have taken the plunge. I knew the one way to do it was to climb right up to the edge and dive in without hesitating. If I hesitated, looked down, looked back, and looked around, I would never make the dive. I felt if I ever hoped to get something started in Mexico City, I could not leave without making a decision and planting the seed.... Before I left, I effectively pushed the button and the light turned green. I told [a local priest] to look for land and suitable contractors.... It had begun.[10]

One hand was on the plow and the other had just written a big check. There could be no looking back. Father Al started to consider which Sisters he would bring back with him to Mexico, where they would remain permanently and take control. It would be in Mexico where he would disappear.

Later that day, a tender and familiar scene took place. Before he was dropped off at Mexico City's airport, Father Al asked a priest to take him back to the Shrine of Our Lady of Guadalupe. There, he fell to his knees and promised Mary he would try his best for her. In his weakened condition, he told her he was still her slave. Perhaps unwittingly to him, the scene unfolded almost identically to the one thirty-three years earlier in Banneux, when in his final days as a seminarian he gave Mary his priesthood.

THEREAFTER, THE AGONY of his interior cross came swiftly. Back in the Far East, he found his body "in something of a physical tailspin". He called his doctor and described his condition. "His advice was to prepare, as it was very possible that in three or four months I would be gone. At the time I had every reason to follow his advice and believe his prediction", Father Al said.[11] Since childhood, he had always had a pure trust in God, but due to the acceleration of ALS, his faith in the Mexican mission seemed to the Sisters to have crescendoed. They

[10] *KMS*, 54.
[11] *KMS*, 74.

saw each day that their spiritual father was fading away, but they also knew he had made a vow to Mary to keep working for her. He had remained obedient to her in weakness.

Father Al made three separate trips to Mexico, where he became a block of pure determination, like the horse Secretariat stretching his lead in Belmont's furious stretch run. If the Sisters of Mary laid roots in Latin America, as Mother Teresa had done in Venezuela in 1965, then Boystowns and Girlstowns could spread to villages throughout Central and South America. Leaning on a cane, he monitored the massive construction site, helped to interview prospective students, hired instructors, and assisted the Sisters in putting out any small procedural fires. He was perhaps most useful as a "pusher", one who would crack the whip on slow-moving subcontractors who had fallen behind on promised construction milestones.

As his work intensified, his suffering increased. At some point in 1991, he had lost the use of his legs and traded in his cane for a wheelchair. Thereafter, like the piecemeal blowing out of votive candles, his body began slowly to cave in on him. Those bold enough to ask how he was holding up were told that he was offering himself as a victim— but even as the word "victim" left his mouth, Father Al wondered if he truly meant it. He shared his thoughts around that time:

> I ask myself, do you really believe that this ALS thing is a gift from God and a grace obtained through the intercession of a dear, departed friend and sister [Saint Thérèse]? Do you really believe what you were saying when you mouthed the prayers of being a victim, like St. Thérèse of Lisieux? Are you playing games and trying to kid people? ... No, what I have written stands. I have expressed as sincerely and candidly as possible what is in my heart.... I continue to struggle and do my best.[12]

As his health deteriorated and he became mostly immobilized, he described the helplessness of a typical day:

> Yesterday, I woke up a little after three in the morning, after a night of mediocre rest. I cannot say that I tossed and turned all night, because tossing and turning are luxuries which are denied the ALS patient.

[12] KMS, 36-37.

You just lie there and do your best to grow quiet and still, relax and rest. My leg hurts and my left shoulder is somewhat painful. My hand is trapped under my leg, and I cannot free it. The room seems very hot. I am perspiring and quite thirsty.

Finally, at 5:15 sharp the long night is over and the door to my room opens, I hear a cheerful "Good morning, Father," from the two sisters who care for me. The sisters get me to the edge of my bed. I sit and my right leg starts doing its morning dance. It is now very spastic and jumps up and down, rather out of control. The sisters help me to my feet.... I must be very cautious, because if at all possible I must avoid another fall. Already in the course of this illness, I have taken five or six bad falls. Each left me a bit bruised and shaken, but, happily, not seriously hurt. However, another fall at this stage of the illness could be quite serious. If I were to break a bone, it would not heal. If I were to strike my head, it could very well be fatal....

The muscles in my neck and shoulders are now quite weak, so that if my head drops it just hangs there, limp on my chest. I have great difficulty in getting it back into an upright position.... Right now, I have very little control over my environment. I have lost all independence and so-called dignity. However, I do not find this all that devastating. I think of Jesus, Lord and Master, who had all power in heaven and earth, yet He deigned to become a small infant. He entrusted Himself totally, to the Virgin of Nazareth. She was free to move Him this way or that way, to dress Him or undress Him, bathe Him, wash Him, and so on. Jesus accepts this with calm serenity and total surrender.... This example of my Lord and Master gives me peace and courage. I try to emulate this example and to let go of any inner resistance. In an easy, relaxed manner, I try to simply go with the flow.

The sisters are angels of mercy. They are patient, caring and very proficient.... It takes about a half hour to get me ready.... Then the sisters leave me alone with the microphone and the recorder. I rehearse my sermon by repeating it again into the mike, which helps me to focus my attention and stimulates my mental faculties. The sisters are back at 6:15, and they push me in the wheelchair to the elevator. We descend from the roof-deck to the ground floor, and then begin the slow journey of about 500 meters to the gymnasium where about 4,000 youngsters have been assembled and are quietly sitting on the floor waiting for Mass to begin. Offering Mass and speaking to the children used to be a consolation, but in the words of the *Imitation of Christ*, "The Lord now has turned into dust all the consolations of the earth." Mass, which used to be consoling, is simply another painful experience and entails a struggle. My pronunciation is very slurred and my voice is so weak. I have to speak with my lips almost kissing the mike....

Occasionally during Mass, flies get into the act and add to the excitement. They play games by landing on my nose, then my forehead, and occasionally my ears or the back of my hands. I wonder if Jesus had a similar form of torture on Calvary. None of the Gospel writers speak of the role of the flies in the Passion of the Christ. But it was hot, it was the middle of the afternoon and there were a lot of people milling about drinking and probably eating. So I imagine there were many flies around also and that some of them added to the torment of the Savior.[13]

Thousands of students and graduates of his Boystowns and Girlstowns planned to gather in Busan in September 1990 to celebrate Father Al's sixtieth birthday. He asked for a single birthday gift: that each attendee remained faithful to their Catholic faith and obliged whatever the Sisters had taught them. He later elaborated:

I asked each graduate to prepare for this special occasion by reviewing his or her spiritual life, getting their religious life in order, and making a good confession. If their marital state was not proper, I asked that they take care of this before my sixtieth birthday. My graduates responded very favorably. They had meetings, spiritual colloquies, and by and large my request had a very positive effect on their overall spiritual and religious life.... So, the disease in my body had a very positive effect on the morale and the spiritual life of my children. They were all doing their very best to live good lives. They were praying as never before. Indeed, I joked, if I had realized what the effect of this illness would have on the day to day lives of my children, even if God did not send it to me in a real manner, I would have invented it long before this.[14]

In the months prior to Father Al's birthday celebrations, hundreds of Boystown and Girlstown students prepared a play based on Father Al's life featuring two of his favorite songs, old-time American classics

[13] KMS, 37–39.
[14] KMS, 93–94.

"Oh, Shenandoah" and "When the Saints Go Marching In", which were performed by a student orchestra. At one point in the play, a student portraying Saint Thérèse of Lisieux left the stage and presented Father Al with a bouquet of roses. Tears welled in his eyes; no one knew that in his illness he had placed the saint as an icon over his heart. In a particular way, he had chosen the Little Flower to accompany him during his bodily crucifixion. Following the festivities, he celebrated a Mass for thousands in the enormous new gymnasium that had just been built.

As the day progressed, Father Al grew tired and asked to be taken back to his bedroom. He asked a Sister to shut the door and to leave him alone in his thoughts. On the way out, he asked that she turn off the light switch. From outside his darkened room, for the first time, a few Sisters thought they heard him crying.

Korean-born Sister Margie Cheong, one of the Sisters Father Al had chosen to help prepare for the opening of the Boystown and Girlstown programs in Mexico, spent much of her days assisting the ailing priest upon his visits to Mexico. She saw the crushing weight of the disease, but also saw a preternatural joy; he had responded to the violence of ALS with a complete embrace of it. It seemed to Sister Margie that Father Al had entered into his immolation as Christ had during his Passion. "When I was helping then, he looked like Christ. I sensed at what I saw that he could be a saint", Sister Margie said. "It was very difficult for him. There was always suffering, but he always smiled and did his best. It seemed the more he suffered for us and for souls, the more graces and blessings came to the children and the Sisters. He had given his suffering to God and to us."

Sister Margie continued: "The closer his end came, as he grew weaker and weaker, the more beautiful his face became. It was an aura. It came from deep within his interior; it was something very spiritually beautiful, something untouchable. He was dying, but he wasn't upset; he was ready." Indeed, he even made the experience consoling for her: "It never was dark throughout the process because of his light. Father Al told us, 'This is just the process I need to go through.' I don't know if he knew it, but he was giving the Sisters and children a hope we hadn't seen before. He was showing us that anything could be accomplished in darkness if it was freely given to Christ."

On October 7, 1991, the feast of Our Lady of the Rosary, Father Al welcomed eight hundred students from the poorest towns of Mexico to their new home. The inauguration of the Boystown and Girlstown in Chalco, a blue-collar town southeast of Mexico City, arrived eighteen months after his pledge to Our Lady of Guadalupe. Before leaving Mexico for the last time, he met with his contractor and told him to begin phase two. Within a year, another seven-story building was added, and eight hundred more of the poor and orphaned from unnamed dirt roads in Oaxaca, Guerrero, Veracruz, Puebla, Mexico City, and villages scattered throughout the countryside were welcomed to Father Al's humble kingdoms of care.

Once he had arrived safely home in the Philippines, Father Al spent his last days entering into what he called his "sacrament of suffering", a sharing in Jesus' own death. His vivid narrative of being nailed to the cross and sharing in the agony of Christ, which he dictated in the last weeks of his life, is worth sharing at length:

> St. Paul writes in one of his Epistles, "With Christ I am nailed to the cross. It is no longer I who live but Christ who lives in me." These were always among my favorite lines from the writings of St. Paul. Now, they have a special, personal, experiential meaning for me. I believe, in all truthfulness, I can now say with St. Paul, with Christ I am nailed to the cross.
>
> There are so many elements of ALS which remind you of the pain of Jesus nailed to the cross.... Jesus was totally disabled and immobilized. His hands and feet were rigidly fixed to the tree so that he could not move. My condition is now the same. I am totally disabled and can no longer move my hands or feet. On the cross, because of His position and the weight of His body, Jesus had great difficulty breathing. In fact, he died of suffocation.... More than likely I will die of suffocation or choking....
>
> Jesus experienced that terrible, overwhelming fatigue which comes from a lack of rest and sleep. He had not slept the night before and he had gone through terrible pain and torture. Because of the lack of oxygen and many other problems which cause insomnia, an ALS patient is always fatigued and experiences terrible sleepiness and drowsiness. Because of an inability to breathe, Jesus spoke very little from the cross.... Most ALS patients, when they die, have lost their ability to speak, not so much from a lack of oxygen as to the fact that

their speaking muscles have atrophied. On the cross, Jesus did not eat or drink.... ALS patients have enormous difficulty in swallowing anything, and as for myself the sight and thought of food repulses and even nauseates me. Also on Calvary, Jesus was stripped of his clothes. He was stripped of his human dignity and lifted up before the world as a spectacle and a laughingstock. I, too, have been stripped of my dignity. Each day is a fresh and new humiliation.

Oh Jesus, forgive me, for what I am going to say, but I am guilty of entertaining the thought, so, I will express it, in all simplicity and candor. At times I looked at your pain and compared it to my own. Then I said, "Your pain lasted only 15 hours or so, from Midnight on Holy Thursday until three on the following Friday afternoon." Indeed, the pain was excruciating, the suffering was horrible, but still the time factor is only 15 hours. If I had my choice of enduring 15 hours of your pain on Calvary in exchange for 15 days of ALS, I would choose the 15 hours of Gethsemane and Calvary. I imagine in my daydreaming 15 days of normal, healthy, active existence. So every 15 days, I would have my hands and my feet pierced and be stretched out on the cross and then the rest of the time I would be free and happy and healthy. It seems to me, if I had my choice, I would choose the cross in exchange for the ALS pain....

[ALS] is relatively clean and odorless. But the most difficult feature, at least for me, with ALS is that it is so terribly slow. It kills, but so softly, so lazily. If it is going to kill you, let it do so quickly and get it over with. But it is like a cat that has caught a mouse and tortures the mouse by playing with it forever. Of course, Lord Jesus, when I speak about exchanging my little pain for your suffering, I do not know what I am talking about. I realize I am speaking nonsense and I ask your pardon. In Scripture, it is written, "Is there any pain like unto my pain?" In reference to the suffering of Jesus the answer to this question is, "No."...

Jesus in His pain and suffering experienced desolation, dryness, and depression in His heart and spirit. Without depression, there is no real pain. Without desolation and despondency, there is no real suffering. So Jesus suffered not only in his flesh but in the very depths of His soul. And he expresses this in His torment in the Garden when he says, "My soul is sorrowful unto death." To paraphrase, "I feel so cut-off and terrible that I would like to die."...

Jesus's role on the cross was to pray and to suffer. He offers to the Father His sacrifice of praise, His prayer together with His terrible pain, with His blood. On the cross, He does not preach. He does not teach. He hardly speaks. On the cross, He performs no miracles. He does not heal. He does not visibly help. He does not plan or organize or do anything productive. Yet, on the cross, by His prayer and suffering, Jesus accomplishes the greatest work in the history of mankind. He redeems the world. He sanctifies man. He obtains salvation for us and nothing more noble, exalted, or holy can be imagined.

My role, now, is more and more similar to that of Jesus on the cross. My productive hour is over. I can hardly talk. I can no longer preach. I have difficulty in doing anything. So my role is simply to offer my prayer and my pain with Jesus to the Father. And this, I think, will be of more benefit to my children, my sisters, [and] my brothers than all of my planning and projects and programs. This is the supreme test and ultimate act of faith and love....

I am nailed to the cross of ALS. Each day the struggle intensifies. The disease is inexorable in its progress. Each day becomes more difficult than the day before, and looking ahead, I see stretching before me uncharted paths of pain, suffering, and humiliation. Being a realist, I am trying to find out how to cope.... The answer is found on Calvary in the person of Jesus. I must aspire to his heroism....

I believe He has sent me ALS as a sign of His love and special favor. I believe this and I try to renew this belief at each instant. So it is, I do not look at ALS as an enemy which I fight. I accept it, embrace it, and welcome it as a friend.... I believe God gives me this pain and suffering. I believe at the same time he gives me the strength and grace to accept it, endure it, and cope with it. Jesus says to St. Paul, "My grace is sufficient for you, my strength is made perfect in your weakness." I believe the grace of Jesus will always be adequate. The problem is, I would like it to be more adequate. But it is enough, just enough, for that moment and that instant. As Jesus on the cross, I do not look back. I do not consider the future but I trust in God. I believe in His grace from instant to instant ....

I believe that suffering is redemptive, pain is salvific, and death and humiliation are fruitful and productive. St. Paul writes, "Without the shedding of blood, there is no work of salvation." And in a similar manner, Jesus in the Gospel says, "Unless a grain of wheat falls into the ground and dies, it remains alone. If it dies, it bears fruit." So, I believe this suffering, humiliation, or pain I endure is purposeful, is fruitful and productive. The blood of Jesus is not enough to redeem the world. He loves us so much, He wants us to participate in the greatest, most satisfying, and fulfilling work imaginable—which is the saving of souls. And, so, He has decreed that all blood must be mingled with the blood of Jesus in order to save and redeem the world. In this Spirit, St. Paul writes, "I make up in my body the sufferings which are lacking in the body of Christ."[15]

FATHER AL SPENT HIS FINAL DAYS living like a poor man in a simple room at the Girlstown community in Manila. He kept his pain silent and listened to a recording of Thérèse of Lisieux's *Last Conversations*, which had become like desert wildflowers for him. The French saint-poet's words, even until the end, were lighting small bonfires of warmth in his body, which had atrophied to less than a hundred pounds. Sister Michaela Kim, to whom he had bequeathed his stewardship as superior general of the Sisters of Mary, was by his side with several other Sisters. In a soft voice, he told his replacement that the Virgin of the Poor did not need him anymore. It was time, he explained to Sister Michaela, that the Virgin worked solely through her and the Sisters of Mary. "He wanted the Sisters to trust in the Virgin of the Poor", Sister Michaela said of his death-bed wishes. "He also repeated many times that the Sisters must be faithful to their three hours of prayer every day.... Until his death he was never depressed.... He never changed his attitude of joyfulness, and he said, 'Although suffering is in me, I am not in it. I am in God.'... [He said that he] was nailed to the cross with Jesus and this would be good for the congregation and the poor."[16]

On March 16, 1992, Father Aloysius Schwartz died peacefully, surrounded by a half dozen of his spiritual daughters. His last words spoke of poverty and of Mary:

> I would be happy with a hole in the ground and a little plaque saying something like this, "Here lies Al Schwartz. He tried his best for Jesus." That's it.... My apostolate is [Mary's] and I would like to be buried at her feet and say, that all praise, honor, and glory for anything good accomplished in my life goes to her and to her alone.[17]

The blood of Venerable Aloysius Schwartz's white martyrdom bore fruit. The Sisters of Mary became as bold as their spiritual father and

[15] *KMS*, 106–8, 110, 117–18.
[16] *Pos*, 136, 615.
[17] *KMS*, 152.

founded Boystowns and Girlstowns in Guatemala, Honduras, Brazil, and Tanzania. As of this writing, more than twenty thousand once-poor souls are being raised to become saints.

FATHER ALOYSIUS SCHWARTZ was declared Venerable by Pope Francis in 2015. It is a title given to those who have lived a life of heroic virtue.

AFTERWORD

by Father Dan Leary

I WAS A FEW YEARS OUT OF VILLANOVA UNIVERSITY and had just finished pretheology at seminary when I found myself at Villa de las Niñas (Girlstown) in Chalco, Mexico, in the summer of 1992. I knew almost nothing about the Sisters of Mary or Aloysius Schwartz, who had just died. Right away, the Sisters began to share stories about their spiritual father's intense love for Mary and how Our Lady had led him to commit his life to saving the poor. When they spoke of him, their eyes blazed. He seemed to me a giant, another Mother Teresa. A priest is ordained to save souls; he had saved generations of souls.

He had just built the Chalco Girlstown while dying of Lou Gehrig's disease. Though he had lost control of his body, the Sisters told me he was hearing more than one hundred confessions a day, celebrating Masses, and giving daily spiritual talks. They spoke of his lifetime of intense prayer, his holiness, his unyielding commitment to asceticism, and of course, his call to the poor. He worked long days and, like Gehrig, refused to take a day off. As a twenty-four-year-old with a simple aim to become a faithful priest, I didn't fully understand the challenge that was being presented to me then, or the impact his priesthood would have on me and all my future parishioners.

All these years later, as God's ways are mysterious, I find myself as a missionary priest here in Mexico on these same life-giving and saving grounds. I write now from my small office not far from where I slept nearly thirty years ago. Outside my room, up a long driveway, there are four enormous buildings where 3,142 teenage girls are sleeping. Down the hallway, 55 Sisters are asleep in their cloister. In July 2020, after serving for twenty-three years as a diocesan priest, my ordinary permitted me to become the chaplain and spiritual director for the Sisters of Mary community. If COVID-19 never happened, I would be traveling to more than 390 Sisters and 20,000 children in the Far East, Africa, and Central and South America.

The immensity of the spiritual work is daunting, but a wise Sister here gave me a great piece of advice. She said, simply, "Father, just do your best. That's all Father Al did."

So like Father Al, I've centered my work here on the spiritual works of mercy. I usually celebrate up to three Masses a day and spend three to five hours each day in the confessional. It seems a time crunch; I often smile to myself when, walking to the confessional, I pass the same long, winding line of kids seeking God's mercy—the same line Father Al passed a half century ago. I also spend many hours each day giving spiritual talks and working to be an instrument of healing in a ministry God is allowing to bear fruit.

This is the most spiritually intense time of my life, but it has also been immensely rewarding. The reason is very simple: daily, I witness the resurrection of children from their afflictions, many of them unspeakable. They are the little "Lazaruses" who step from their tombs, most of them, for the first time. There is a stunning vulnerability in how they open to me their stories of pain to begin the long process of healing. Their courage often leaves me wordless. I've heard stories that have stunned me and brought me to tears, but I've also found just as staggering their strength to enter into a healing process that is so often gut-wrenching—but always, in the end, liberating. Countless teenagers have begun their journey toward healing by asking, "Father, may I open my pain to you?" Many write letters to those who have haunted and hurt them in unthinkable ways. But with the grace of God, they rip up the letters and dispose of them at the base of the monstrance during Adoration. They adore Christ in the Eucharist and daily pray the Rosary at seven P.M.—oftentimes simply begging Jesus and Mary to help them detach from their memories. Then, as Christ begins to cleanse, sanctify, and deliver them from their wounds, they start to live. It is remarkable the number of times I've heard the same question asked in the process of their recovery: "Father, how can I be holy now?"

For more than a half century, the Sisters of Mary have traveled to the poorest communities in the world to receive children from families to give them the chance to grow in the love of Christ and the Church and break the cycle of poverty. After five years, the children are sent back to their families as reborn Catholic missionaries, where they help to rebuild their families and communities as resurrected souls. It is of the Holy Spirit.

After Father Al's passing, the Sisters of Mary pushed forward with his work in Korea and the Philippines. They have since finished his expansion into Mexico and, through the grace of God, opened new Girlstowns and Boystowns in Guatemala, Brazil, Honduras, and Tanzania. These Boystowns and Girlstowns throughout the world have become, I believe, a large part of the future Catholic Church. Because Father Al and the Sisters strove to give them the best care, catechesis, and formation, the children leave as bold witnesses of Christ in the world. Truly, I've worked with teenage boys and girls who want to become saints, which presses me harder as a priest. The Sisters are forming the next generation of Catholics—strong Catholics—but just as vitally, they are forming rebuilders. These graduates leave with an intense, burning desire to love Christ and serve others in their own poor villages and beyond.

I truly believe that both the graduates and those who support the work of the Sisters are carrying much of the future of the Catholic Church on their shoulders. The light of goodness, truth, and stripped-down beauty will heal the Church and cast out the darkness—and the Sisters of Mary's charitable work is a beacon of light that radiates.

At a time when Christians are straining to find true witnesses, when people are searching for hope in a beleaguered Church and world, I do not think there is anything comparable to the work of the Sisters of Mary. Father Al said, "A poverty-inspired Church which goes primarily to the poor is a Church of miracles."

Following in the steps of a saint (not yet canonized, though) is hard—and yet at the same time, it is simple. It's difficult because of Father Al's immense spiritual gifts on a multitude of levels. It is undeniable that the Virgin of the Poor worked through him in many, many ways. But it is also relatively easy because Father Al showed me how to serve the community. His life confirmed in me the manner of the priesthood. He laid the foundation, built it, formed the Sisters, heard the cry of Our Lady to care for the poor, and gave children the opportunity to step away from the cycle of poverty. My ministry is simply continuing to serve the poor in the mission that God put on Father Al's heart. Now, the mission is in mine.

The Sisters continue this profound mission of bringing Christ to the poor, and then the poor bring Christ to others. I can't explain to you how vital this simple model is in these often dark days. Thus, these young saints-to-be are now given the tools they need to dig themselves out of poverty and to lead countless others to encounter Jesus Christ and the fullness of the truth.

I knew nothing of this mission twenty-eight years ago, but now believe it to be the most important in this world.

Father Al needs a few miracles to become canonized as a saint in the Church. His work, though, speaks for itself. It is the work of God. It is a miracle of God.

Rest in peace, my brother priest in Christ, and pray for us. Your spiritual children haven't forgotten you, Father Al; in fact many want to become you.

To learn more about Venerable Aloysius Schwartz or the work of the Sisters of Mary, visit thesistersofmary.org or call 1-800-662-6316.

PRAYER FOR THE BEATIFICATION
OF ALOYSIUS SCHWARTZ

Almighty, ever-living God, giver of all good gifts, you have filled
Monsignor Al with an ardent love for you and for souls. You have
inspired him to dedicate his life to relieve the suffering of the orphans,
abandoned, the sick, and the poor, especially the youth, which he did
with all humility and courage until the end of his life.

May his holy life of love and service to the poor be recognized by
the Church through his beatification and canonization and be my
inspiration to strive for perfection in the love of God and service to
others. We ask this through the merits of our Lord Jesus Christ and
the prayers of Mary, the Virgin of the Poor. Amen.

Our Father. Hail Mary. Glory Be.